Classroom Science from A to Z

26 Complete Classroom Lessons

Mickey Sarquis and Lynn Hogue

Terrific Science Press
Miami University Middletown
Middletown, Ohio

Millburn C. C. School District 24
18550 Millburn Road
Wadsworth, IL 60083

Terrific Science Press
Miami University Middletown
4200 East University Blvd.
Middletown, Ohio 45042
513/727-3269
www.terrificscience.org

10   9   8   7   6   5   4   3

ISBN 1-883822-22-X

This material is based, in part, upon work supported by the National Science Foundation under grant number ESI-9355523 and a grant under the federally funded Dwight D. Eisenhower Mathematics and Science Education Act, administered by the Ohio Board of Regents. Any opinions, findings, and conclusions or recommendations expressed in this material are those of the authors and do not necessarily reflect the views of the funding agencies.

Contents

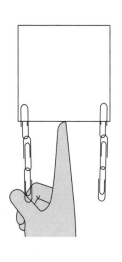

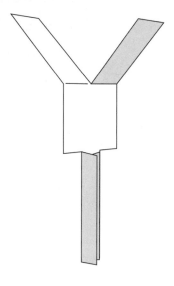

Acknowledgments

The authors wish to thank the following individuals and organizations who have contributed to the development of the activities in this book.

Contributors

Mary Jo Gardner	Fairmont Egan Elementary School	Kalispell, MT
Paula Halm	Heritage Hills Elementary School	Cincinnati, OH
Bev Kutsunai	Kamehameha Elementary School	Honolulu, HI
Phil McBride	Eastern Arizona College	Thatcher, AZ
Veronica Newman	Oakdale Elementary School	Cincinnati, OH
Mary Neises	Bauer Elementary School	Miamisburg, OH
Dwight Portman	Winton Woods High School	Cincinnati, OH
Cynthia Stanford	Norwood View Elementary School	Cincinnati, OH
Linda Woodward	Center for Chemical Education	Middletown, OH

Support for the Development of this Book

This book was developed in conjunction with the Teaching Science with TOYS program through the support of the National Science Foundation and the Ohio Board of Regents. The goals of Teaching Science with TOYS are to enhance teachers' knowledge of chemistry and physics and to encourage activity-based, discovery-oriented science through the use of toys and other everyday objects.

Terrific Science Press Design and Production Team

Document Production Manager: Susan Gertz

Technical Coordinator: Lisa Taylor

Technical Writing: Lisa Taylor, Susan Gertz, Christine Mulvin, Amy Hudepohl

Technical Editing: Amy Stander, Lisa Taylor, Christine Mulvin

Book Illustration: Carole Katz

Photo Editing: Brian Fair

Design/Layout: Susan Gertz

Production: Christine Mulvin, Becky Franklin, Stephen Gentle, Amy Hudepohl, Lisa Taylor, Jennifer Stencil, Brian Fair

Laboratory Testing: Eric Buck

Reviewers

Frank Cardulla	Niles North High School (retired)	Skokie, IL
Herman Keith	The Kinkaid School/Univ. of Houston	Houston, TX
Dwight Portman	Winton Woods High School	Cincinnati, OH
J. Timothy Perry	Mt. Hebron High School	Ellicott City, MD
Jerry Sarquis	Miami University	Oxford, OH
Beverley A.P. Taylor	Miami University Hamilton	Hamilton, OH

Testers

Family teams at Kamehameha School, Honolulu, Hawaii

Family teams at Central Academy, Middletown, OH

Teaching Science with TOYS Participants, 1998–1999

Chad Agnes	Lorin Andrews Middle School	Massillon, OH
Briana Ainsworth	MonDay Community Correctional Institute	Dayton, OH
Susan Alexander	Washington Elementary	Hillsboro, OH
Deborah Arndts	Twin Valley Local	West Alexandria, OH
Jennifer Arnold	Willowville Elementary	Batavia, OH
Joanne Ashworth	Monroe Elementary	Monroe, OH
Dianna Bartles	W.M. Sellman School	Madeira, OH
Pam Bennington	Vernon Primary	Wheelersburg, OH
Sheri Benton	Maineville Elementary	Maineville, OH
Karen Blackmon	Van Buren Elementary	Hamilton, OH
Sister M. Joletta Boellner	St. Wendelin Elementary	Fostoria, OH
Gerri Bolin	C.O. Harrison Elementary	Cincinnati, OH
Sheryl Borger	Laura Farrell School	Franklin, OH
Ladonna Boyd	Alexander Elementary School	Albany, OH
Rita Brown	Union Furnace Elementary	Union Furnace, OH
Virginia Browne	Lemoyne Elementary	Lemoyne, OH
Jennifer Brunka	Roselawn-Condon	Cincinnati, OH
Linda Campbell	Lynchburg Elementary/Junior High	Lynchburg, OH
Kathleen Carpenter	Ada Exempted Village Schools	Ada, OH
Toni Cary	Valley Elementary	Beavercreek, OH
Peg Cassaro	Our Lady of Lourdes	Cincinnati, OH
Holly Chakeres	Groveport Madison Middle School-North	Columbus, OH
Bonita Cochran	Valley Elementary	Beavercreek, OH
Mandy Cole	Struble Elementary	Cincinnati, OH
Tanya Cordes	Swifron Primary	Cincinnati, OH
E. Lee Cornett	Three Rivers Middle School	Cleves, OH
Julie Cowan	Van Buren Elementary	Hamilton, OH
Kelly Craig	Clearcreek Elementary	Stoutsville, OH
Jocelyn Crawford	Main Elementary School	Beavercreek, OH
Kathy Damron	College Hill Fundamental Academy	Cincinnati, OH
Diana Davis	Amelia Middle School	Batavia, OH
Barbara DeBolt	Green Elementary Logan	Logan, OH
Anne Demmel	Ann Weigel Elementary	Cincinnati, OH
Joanne DeTomaso	Bellcreek Elementary	Bellbrook, OH
Karen Develen	St. Bernard Elementary	St. Bernard, OH
Erica Devol	Central Elementary Logan	Logan, OH
Drew Dilley	Three Rivers Middle School	Cleves, OH
JoAnna Dorman	Hartwell Elementary	Cincinnati, OH
Lonnie Dusch	Mt. Healthy High School	Cincinnati, OH
Deborah Dye	New Miami Elementary	Hamilton, OH
Janice Eberle	Evamere Primary School	Hudson, OH
Kimberly Eibel	South Amherst M.S.	South Amherst, OH
Susan Eichel	C.O. Harrison Elementary	Cincinnati, OH
Mary Etter	Our Lady of Lourdes	Cincinnati, OH
Connie Fleming	East Elementary School	Logan, OH
Diana Flood	Green Elementary School	Logan, OH
Vicki Floyd	Green Elementary School	Franklin Furnace, OH
Catherine Frazier	Wm. H. Taft Elementary School	Cincinnati, OH
Jan French	Cincinnati Country Day	Cincinnati, OH
Susan Freund	Monroe Elementary	Monroe, OH
David Fugate	Heritage Elementary	West Chester, OH
Nancy Galusha	J.E. Prass Elementary	Kettering, OH
Janice Gault	Logan-Hocking Middle School	Logan, OH
John Gilpin	Conneaut High School	Conneaut, OH
Elke Gies	C.O. Harrison Elementary	Cincinnati, OH

Paige Gipson	Norwood Middle School	Norwood, OH
Cathy Girard	St. Rita School for the Deaf	Cincinnati, OH
Joanna Goldslager	Mason Heights Elementary School	Mason, OH
Roderick Gray	Meadowdale H.S.	Dayton, OH
Ginger Hamm	St. Cecilia School	Cincinnati, OH
Sheila Harris	Harrisonville Elementary	Pomeroy, OH
Tamiko Hatcher	Lehman Middle School	Canton, OH
Kimberly Hayes	East Elementary School	Logan, OH
Delores Heffner	St. Cecilia School	Cincinnati, OH
Lee Hieber	Fairfield City Schools, East Elementary	Hamilton, OH
Steven Hoffman	Clearcreek Elementary	Springboro, OH
Sheila Holbrock	Monroe Elementary	Monroe, OH
Cynthia Hopkins	Madeira City Schools	Cincinnati, OH
Deborah Howard	Adams Elementary School	Hamilton, OH
Kimberly Howard	Vernon Primary	Wheelersburg, OH
Randall Hoying	St. Henry High School	St. Henry, OH
Mary Ann Hughes	Union Furnace Elementary	Union Furnace, OH
Anbela Isaacs	Lincoln Elementary School	Hamilton, OH
Marcie Janey	Central Elementary Logan	Logan, OH
Sandra Kalisewicz	Middletown/Monroe School District	Monroe, OH
Sharon Keplar	Green Elementary Logan	Logan, OH
Linda Kraus	East Elementary	Greenville, OH
Ann Krentz	Mason Heights Elementary School	Mason, OH
Brenda Kurtz	J. F. Dulles Elementary/Oak Hills S.D.	Cincinnati, OH
Marianne Ladenburger	Clough Pike Elementary	Cincinnati, OH
Timmiera Lawrence	Lloyd Mann Primary	Loveland, OH
Gena Leisten	Hamilton-Maineville Elementary	Maineville, OH
Margaret Libecap	Westbrook Elementary	Brookville, OH
Vivian Liette	Ansonia High School	Ansonia, OH
Patricia Lillibridge	Lincoln Elementary School	Hamilton, OH
Mary Malone	McKinley Kindergarden Center-Hamilton	Hamilton, OH
Suzanne Martin	Lemoyne Elementary	Lemoyne, OH
Amy Mayer	Cherokee Elementary	Hamilton, OH
Holly McElwee	South Elementary School	Greenville, OH
Lorrie McGuire	Trimble Elementary	Glouster, OH
Sharon Meek	Green Elementary	Franklin Furnace, OH
Cheryl Miller	Pennyroyal Elementary	Franklin, OH
Lisa Miller	Harrisonville Elementary	Pomeroy, OH
Michelle Miller	New Miami Elementary	Hamilton, OH
Phyllis Miller	Twin Valley Schools	West Alexandria, OH
Charlotte Moore	Vernon Primary	Wheelersburg, OH
Sheryl Morrison	Garfield Jr. High	Hamilton, OH
Patricia Neyer	C.O. Harrison Elementary	Cincinnati, OH
Daniel Nieman	Ursuline Academy	Cincinnati, OH
Sharon Orsi	Westbrook Elementary	Brookville, OH
Rebecca Osburn	Union Furnace Elementary	Union Furnace, OH
Melissa Parsons	Norwood Middle School	Norwood, OH
Joan Pierce	MonDay Community Correctional Institute	Dayton, OH
Gwen Pleiman	West Carrollton Junior High School	West Carrollton, OH
Stephanie Quiett	Garfield Jr. High	Hamilton, OH
Marsha Radabaugh	Middleport Elementary	Middleport, OH
Teresa Reynolds	Willowville Elementary	Batavia, OH
Jo Ann Rigano	Valley Elementary	Beavercreek, OH
Julie Rush	McAuley High School	Cincinnati, OH
Patricia Scherff	Spaulding Middle School	Goshen, OH
Diana Schwartz	J.A. Garfield Middle School	Garrettsville, OH
Mary Scott	Evamere Primary School	Hudson, OH 44236
Candace Sharp	Vandalia-Butler City Schools	Vandalia, OH
Karen Sides	Fairfield City Schools- East Elementary	Hamilton, OH
Sandra Slobodzian-Zipes	E.D. Smith Elementary School	Dayton, OH
Jamee Sprengard	Bridgetown Jr. High School	Cincinnati, OH
Robert Starkey	Conneaut Area School	Conneaut, OH

Joan Stidham	Indian Hill Elementary	Cincinnati, OH
Kathy Stotts	Green Elementary Logan	Logan, OH
Elizabeth Stratman	Hartwell School	Cincinnati, OH
Julie Stueve	Kitty Hawk	Huber Heights, OH
Ken Sturgill	Wilson Jr. High School	Hamilton, OH
Patty Sutton	Indian Hill Elementary	Cincinnati, OH
Sonya Tennant	Allensville Elementary	McArthur, OH
Cheryl Turner	Amelia Middle School	Batavia, OH
Kelly Turner	Fillmore Elementary	Hamilton, OH
Carol Umberg	St. Bernard Elementary	St. Bernard, OH
Janice Vanderplough	St. Jospeh Orphanage	Cincinnati, OH
Karen Veidt	Green Elementary Logan	Logan, OH
Kelli Wagner	J.F. Dulles Elementary	Cincinnati, OH
Kathy Wallen	Washington Elementary	Hillsboro, OH
Patricia Ward	Monroe Elementary	Monroe, OH
Rebecca Ward	Jefferson Elementary	Middletown, OH
Darlene West	Delhi Junior High School	Cincinnati, OH
Amy White	Hamilton-Maineville Elementary	Maineville, OH
Linda Willard	Green Elementary Logan	Logan, OH
Wilson Willard III	R.E. Lucas Intermediate School	Cincinnati, OH
Peggy Williams	Bellcreek Elementary	Bellbrook, OH
Robin Willis	Swifton Primary	Cincinnati, OH
Jo Ann Wingereid	Mason Heights Elementary	Mason, OH
Kathleen Wirsch	St. John The Baptist School	Harrison, OH
Patricia Witson	Shroder Paideia Middle School	Cincinnati, OH
Leslie Yinger	Coolville Elementary	Coolville, OH
Karen Zearbaugh	Batavia Middle School	Batavia, OH

Foreword

Science doesn't have to be intimidating, and it certainly should never be boring. You can help your students discover the excitement of scientific exploration for themselves with this collection of hands-on activities. *Classroom Science from A to Z* is a valuable teacher resource of standards-based science lessons for the elementary level. The book includes 26 physical science lessons, one for each letter of the alphabet. Each lesson provides links to the National Science Education Standards and includes one or more science activities with reproducible student handouts, teacher notes for setup, assessment suggestions, cross-curricular ideas, and a complete, easy-to-understand explanation of the science involved.

The science activities in this book use simple toys and everyday objects familiar to students, such as paper clips, pencils, and mirrors. Activities based on such familiar and friendly objects will help students understand that science is always a part of their world.

You can enhance the classroom experience with family fun using the companion to this book, *Science Night Family Fun from A to Z.* The activities in *Science Night Family Fun from A to Z* coordinate by science topic and alphabetical letter with the lessons in this book, but they are designed specifically for a family science event setting. A family science event is a wonderful way to encourage family involvement in education.

We think you'll find that the lessons in this book will give a lift to science in your classroom and make science more interesting relevant, and fun—both to learn and to teach. Good luck, and have fun!

Mickey Sarquis, Director
Center for Chemical Education

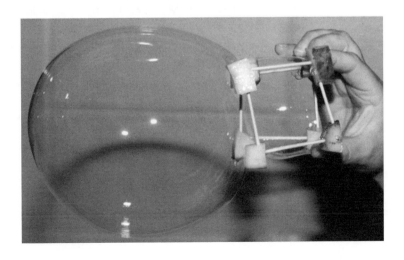

Getting the Most from This Book

Classroom Science from A to Z was developed to be a valuable resource for standards-based elementary-level science education. The classroom lessons in this book are presented by chapter in alphabetical order.

This book was also designed to be a companion to *Science Night Family Fun from A to Z,* a collection of hands-on science activities designed for use in a family science event. The lessons in *Classroom Science from A to Z* can help turn a one-time family science event into a springboard for a longer-term learning experience. Each lesson coordinates with the Family Science Challenge that begins with the same letter of the alphabet.

The rest of "Getting the Most From This Book" describes the items in each chapter that will help you prepare and conduct your lessons.

Introductory Page

Each chapter begins with an introductory page that gives a quick overview of the lesson by providing the following information:

- statement describing the link to the related activity in *Science Night Family Fun from A to Z,*
- description of the lesson,
- table of contents for the lesson components,
- key science topics addressed in the lesson, and
- time required for the activity (the time needed to set up the activity, perform the activity, and clean up afterward).

National Science Education Standards

To help you coordinate your lessons with the National Science Education Standards, the National Science Education Standards Matrix in the back of this book provides an overview of how the lessons in this book and the related activities in *Science Night Family Fun from A to Z* coordinate with the standards. For more detailed information, each lesson provides a listing of the relevant standards along with brief descriptions of how different facets of the lessons and activities coordinate with the standards. Since this book and *Science Night Family Fun from A to Z* are designed for all elementary levels, some of the standards statements apply to the K–4 level and others apply to the 5–8 level. The following is an example of standards statements from Lesson C, "Counterrevolution":

Science as Inquiry Standards

- Abilities Necessary to Do Scientific Inquiry

  Students conduct a simple investigation of the helicopter and make systematic observations of the effects that folding and adding paper clips have on the helicopter's flight.

  Students construct reasonable explanations of the effects that folding and adding paper clips have on the helicopter's flight.

Physical Science

- Position and Motion of Objects

  The motion of the helicopter can be described by its position, direction of motion, and speed.

  Objects with blades or wings tend to rotate as they fall.

  Unbalanced forces will cause changes in the speed, direction, and rotation of the helicopter's motion.

Science and Technology

- Abilities of Technological Design

  Students discuss the characteristics of a superior whirligig design.

  In the Assessment, students design and conduct a set of experiments to investigate variables that affect the flight of the helicopter.

  Students present their conclusions to their classmates.

Science Activity Handout(s)

The science activity handouts are designed to be read and used by the students. Each Science Activity handout contains a challenge for students and complete instructions for the activity. You may photocopy these handouts for classroom use.

Teacher Notes for the Science Activity

Teacher Notes are provided for each Science Activity. Teacher Notes may include all or some of the following elements:

- Materials list
- Resources—describes where to obtain any unusual or hard-to-find items in the Materials list
- Safety—describes special safety precautions, if any, that should be taken during the activity
- Setup—explains how to get ready for the activity
- Disposal—describes any special procedures, if necessary, for disposing of products or materials after the activity

- Answers and Observations—offers plausible answers for questions on the student activity handout (When the question calls for a prediction or for observations that may vary greatly, sometimes answers are not provided.)
- Suggestions for Follow-Up—contains ideas for discussing results and exploring further

Assessment

Assessment and learning are two sides of the same coin. Assessments enable students to let teachers know what they are learning, and when students engage in an assessment exercise, they should learn from it. Ideally, assessments maximize the opportunity for all students to demonstrate their accomplishments and understanding. To this end, each lesson in this book provides a suggested activity-based assessment idea.

Science Explanation

Each lesson provides a clear, complete science explanation that covers the science activity in the classroom lesson, the related activity in *Science Night Family Fun from A to Z*, and the assessment activity. To help you gain a deeper understanding of the topic, the explanations provide more detail than we expect you to give your students. You are encouraged to modify the discussion as necessary for your own students.

Cross-Curricular Integration

Cross-curricular integration can extend the excitement and impact of science learning into many other areas. This section contains ideas for integrating the science presented in the lesson with the following subject areas:
- Art and Music
- Earth Science
- Home, Safety, and Career
- Language Arts
- Life Science
- Mathematics
- Physical Education
- Social Studies
- Just for Fun

The World Wide Web is also an excellent resource for discovering links between science and the areas listed here. Consider having your students conduct web searches as part of the lessons in this book by providing them with suggested search words and phrases.

Be Careful—and Have Fun!

The hands-on science investigations in this book will add fun and excitement to science education in your classroom. However, even the simplest activity can become dangerous when the proper safety precautions are ignored, when the activity is done incorrectly, or when the activity is performed by students without proper supervision. The science investigations in this book have been extensively reviewed by classroom teachers of elementary grades and by university scientists. We have done all we can to assure the safety of the activities as written. It is up to you to assure their safe execution!

- Always practice activities yourself before performing them with your class. This is the only way to become thoroughly familiar with the procedures and materials required for an activity, and familiarity will help prevent potentially hazardous (or merely embarrassing) mishaps. In addition, you may find variations that will make the activity more meaningful to your students.

- Read each activity carefully and observe all safety precautions and disposal procedures.

- Special safety instructions are not given for everyday classroom materials being used in a typical manner. Use common sense when working with hot, sharp, or breakable objects, such as flames, scissors, or glassware. Keep tables or desks covered to avoid stains. Clean up spills to prevent falls.

- In some activities, potentially hazardous items such as hot-melt glue guns are to be used only by the teacher.

- When introducing an activity that involves smelling potentially unknown odors, instruct the students about protecting themselves. Tell them never to smell an unknown substance by placing it directly under the nose. Show the students how to use the wafting procedure (explained below) and remind them to avoid prolonged inhalation of objectionable odors—such odors are typically not good for us. If an odor cannot be detected through wafting, the material can be waved closer to the nose.

To smell unknown odors, hold the container approximately 6 inches from the nose and, using the free hand, gently waft the air above the open container toward the nose. (See Figure 1.)

Use your free hand to gently fan the vapors from the test tube toward your nose.

Figure 1: Show your students how to use the wafting procedure to smell unknown odors.

Abracadabra

Enrich the "Aquatic Action" activity in the book Science Night Family Fun from A to Z *or use as a stand-alone lesson on siphons.*

Students investigate how siphons work and make a special siphon called a Tantalus Cup.

. . . . ## Key Science Topics

- atmospheric pressure
- gravity
- siphons
- water pressure

. . . . ## Average Time Required

Science Activity 1		Science Activity 2	
Setup	10 minutes	Setup	15–20 minutes
Performance	10–15 minutes	Performance	15–25 minutes
Cleanup	5 minutes	Cleanup	5 minutes

. . . . **National Science Education Standards**

Science as Inquiry Standards

- Abilities Necessary to Do Scientific Inquiry
  Students use their observations of their siphon and of water within a tube to construct an explanation for the observations and to solve problems.

  Students use their observations to develop cause-and-effect relationships to explain unexpected results.

  Students share their observations with their adult partners and with their classmates.

Physical Science

- Position and Motion of Objects
  Siphons work because water is pushed by the pressure differences that result from different heights of liquids.

- Motions and Forces
  Unbalanced pressures cause changes in the motion of water in a tube.

Science and Technology

- Abilities of Technological Design
  Students compare and contrast a simple overflow device and a Tantalus Cup (a type of siphon) based on the purposes and designs of the devices.

History and Nature of Science

- Science as a Human Endeavor
  Siphons, including the Tantalus Cup, have had practical uses for thousands of years.

Science Activity 1

Materials

2 pieces of clear, flexible plastic tubing with different diameters
• bucket of colored water • paper towels

Challenge

Can you defy gravity using a water-filled tube?

Procedure

Figure 1

Figure 2

❶ Submerge the entire piece of thin plastic tubing in the bucket of colored water. While the tubing is submerged, move it around in the water to remove any air that may be trapped in it.

❷ Use your thumb or finger to completely cover one end of the tubing while it is still in the water. (See Figure 1.) Keeping your finger tightly over that end of the tubing, raise the end up and out of the bucket and then continue to lift until the entire tube is out of the bucket. (See Figure 2.) Keep the tube over the bucket, just in case.

? *What happens to the water in the tube?*

_____

_____

_____

❸ While still holding the tubing over the bucket, remove your finger from the closed end.

? *What happens? Why might this have happened?*

_____

_____

_____

❹ Repeat steps 1–3 with the thick plastic tubing.

? *What happens?*

_____

_____

_____

Figure 3

❺ Refill one of the pieces of tubing with water as you did in step 1. While both ends of the tubing are still underwater, place your finger tightly over one end of the tubing, and have your partner place his or her finger tightly over the other end of the tubing. (See Figure 3.) Lift the tubing carefully out of the water without removing your fingers.

❻ Work over the bucket so that if any water spills it will fall into the bucket and not onto the floor. Hold the tubing so that it looks like the letter "U." (See Figure 4.) Both you and your partner should now remove your fingers from over the ends while continuing to hold the tubing in the "U" shape.

? *What do you observe?*

_____

_____

_____

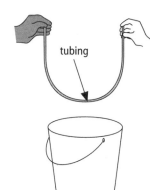

tubing

Figure 4

❼ Slowly lower one side of the tubing so the tubing looks like a "J." Bring the lowered end back to its original level to form a "U" again.

? *What do you observe?*

_____

_____

_____

Science Activity 2

Materials

2 stoppers with tubing attached • tall funnel made from a 2-L bottle • pop-beaker with several holes or slits around the middle, made from a 2-L bottle • pitcher or other container of water

Challenge

Can you determine how an overflow device and a Tantalus Cup are similar and how they are different?

Procedure

❶ Push the stopper with the short flexible tubing into the funnel, with the tubing extending upward. (See Figure 1.)

❷ Place the funnel in the pop-beaker as shown in Figure 2.

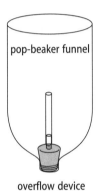

pop-beaker funnel

overflow device

Figure 1

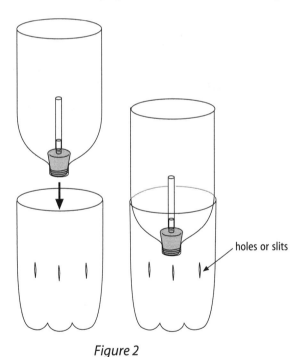

holes or slits

Figure 2

❸ Slowly pour water into the funnel, stopping just below the top of the tubing. Predict what will happen if you add more water. Then try it and record your observations.

Prediction: _____

Observation: _____

_____

❹ Empty the water from the bottom container. Remove the stopper and tubing from the funnel. Push the second stopper (with the longer tubing on it) into the funnel. Bend the tubing as shown in Figure 3.

❺ Slowly pour water into the funnel, stopping just under the bend in the tubing. Predict what will happen if you pour more water into the funnel. Then try it and record your observations.

Prediction: _____

Observation: _____

_____

Tantalus Cup

Figure 3

❻ In steps 1–3, you made an overflow device. In steps 4–5, you made a Tantalus Cup. Now, make each device again and take a closer look as the water moves through each device.

Teacher Notes
for Science Activity 1

Materials

For Setup only
• heavy-duty scissors or a sharp knife

Per group
• piece of clear plastic tubing approximately 18 inches long with an inside diameter of ¼–⅜ inch
• piece of clear plastic tubing approximately 18 inches long with an inside diameter ⅝-inch or greater
• bucket
• water
• paper towels

Resources

• The bucket should be large enough to submerge the tubing completely and allow two students to reach inside and grab the ends of the tubing at the same time.

• Clear, flexible tubing is available from pet stores in the aquarium section, or from hardware stores or science supply houses.

Safety

If water spillage is a problem in the classroom, this activity can be done as a demonstration or done outside. Only the teacher should cut the tubing.

Setup

• Half-fill the buckets with water.

• If the tubing is not already cut, use a sharp knife or heavy-duty scissors to cut it to length.

Answers and Observations

❷ *What happens to the water in the tube?*

The water remains in the tube.

❸ *What happens? Why might this have happened?*

The water runs out of the tubing. This happens because air can now enter the open end to replace the water as it flows out.

❹ *What happens?*

The water runs out of the tubing.

❻ *What do you observe?*

The water remains in the tubing.

❼ *What do you observe?*

Water flows out of the low side of the "J" until the water is the same height on both sides of the "J." When the tubing is returned to the "U" shape, the water level is still the same on both sides of the "U," but the water level is lower.

Suggestion for Follow-Up

As a class, discuss students' observations regarding the water in the tube. Have students predict the results of using the second piece of tubing to repeat steps 5–7 of Science Activity 1. Then let them try it and see if they observe any differences.

Teacher Notes for Science Activity 2

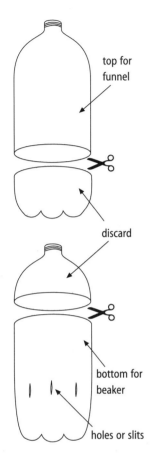

top for funnel

discard

bottom for beaker

holes or slits

Figure 1

Materials

For Setup only
- heavy-duty scissors or a sharp knife
- vegetable oil or water (to use as a lubricant)

Per group
- tall funnel made from a 2-L plastic soft-drink bottle (See Setup.)
- tall beaker made from a 2-L plastic soft-drink bottle (See Setup.)
- 2 stopper and tubing assemblies, each made from the following (See Setup.)
  - 1-hole stopper
  - piece of rigid tubing 3 inches long
  - piece of clear, flexible tubing (one 3-inch piece and one 8-inch piece)
- pitcher or other container for pouring water
- water

Safety

Only the teacher should cut the 2-L bottles and tubing. Take care not to impale your hand when putting the rigid tubing into the stopper.

Setup

rigid tubing

1-hole stopper

Figure 2

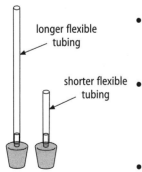

longer flexible tubing

shorter flexible tubing

Figure 3

- Use sharp scissors or a sharp knife to carefully cut two different 2-L bottles in half as shown in Figure 1.
- Cut 6–8 slits (2–3 cm long) in the plastic beaker, evenly spaced around the middle as shown in Figure 1.
- Cut the tubing into the lengths required: rigid tubing, 3 inches; flexible tubing, 3 and 8 inches.
- Lubricate the holes of the stoppers with a little vegetable oil or water. Insert a piece of rigid plastic tubing through each hole. (See Figure 2.) Be careful not to push the tubing into your hand.
- Add a short piece of flexible tubing to the rigid tubing at the top of half the stoppers. Add a long piece of flexible tubing to the rest. (See Figure 3.) It may help to lubricate the outside of the rigid tubing with a little vegetable oil or water to help the flexible tubing slide on more easily.
- Fill the pitchers or other containers with water. The pitcher of water should not be too heavy for students to lift easily.

Answers and Observations

3 *Observation:*

The water above the top of the tubing runs out of the funnel through the tubing.

5 *Observation:*

Once the water level in the funnel is above the bend in the tubing, water begins to flow through the tubing and out of the funnel. It continues to flow out until the water level in the funnel falls below the open end of the tubing inside the funnel.

Suggestions for Follow-Up

Have the class discuss the similarities and differences between the overflow device and the Tantalus Cup that were used in this activity. *Both the overflow device and the Tantalus Cup limit the height of the water in the funnel. However, the Tantalus Cup is a siphon, but the overflow device is not.*

Assessment

Materials

For Setup only
- drill

Per Demonstration
- opaque plastic pitcher
- piece of clear plastic flexible tubing long enough to form a loop inside the pitcher
- water
- bucket

Tantalus pitcher

Setup

You will need to make a tantalus pitcher for this activity as described below:

- Drill a hole in the side of the pitcher at the bottom that is just large enough to insert the tubing. The tubing must fit very snugly in the hole or water will leak during the activity.
- Bend the tubing into an oval shape, and insert one end of the tubing through the hole as shown in the figure.
- Fill the pitcher with water to just below the top of the bend in the tubing.

Demonstration

❶ Place the "Tantalus Pitcher" on the edge of a desk or table so that the students can't see the water or tubing inside it but they can see that there is a hole in the side of the pitcher.

❷ Ask students how much water should come out of the pitcher if one cup is added. Add a cup of water (enough so the water level will be higher than the bend in the tube) to the pitcher.

❸ Hold the cup beneath the hole to catch the water that comes out. Be sure to have a bucket to catch the rest of the water that will come out of the pitcher.

Challenge

After doing the demonstration, challenge the students to explain how it worked. Without letting them look at the apparatus, have them use what they have learned about siphons to draw a picture of what the inside of the pitcher probably looks like. Explain that the pitcher is called a "Tantalus Pitcher," from the word "tantalize." Define "tantalize," and ask students why they think the pitcher has this name. End by having the students write one important fact or idea they learned in this lesson in their science journals.

Science Explanation

This section explains the science concepts in this lesson as well as in the "Aquatic Action" Family Science Challenge in Science Night Family Fun from A to Z. *It is intended for the teacher's information and may be modified as necessary for discussion with students.*

A siphon is a device with which liquid is pushed up and then deposited at a lower level. To create a simple siphon, a tube (usually flexible) is first filled with liquid and then positioned in an inverted "U" shape (or "J" shape) so that one end is in a container of liquid and the other end is outside and lower than the liquid level in the container.

A simple siphon works because of gravity's pull on the water in the tubing and the difference in total pressure (water pressure plus atmospheric pressure) on each side. The water pressure is caused by gravity's pull on the water in the tubing above each side of the siphon. The water pressure changes as you move one side of the tubing up or down. Atmospheric pressure is produced because gravity pulls the mass of the matter that makes up the atmosphere toward the Earth's surface. Although atmospheric pressure can change with altitude or with the weather, it will generally remain constant during the time period of this activity.

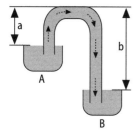

If "b" is higher than "a," the water flows from "A" to "B" as indicated by the arrows.

Figure 1

Figure 1 illustrates the movement of water in a simple siphon where the height of the water on side B is greater than the height of the water on side A. Gravity pulls down on the water in both sides of the tubing. If the water were to empty out of side A, it would be flowing counterclockwise as it moved into side B. If water were to empty out of side B, it would be flowing clockwise as it moved into side A. Water cannot flow out of both sides at once, because that would leave a vacuum in the tube. Figure 1 shows that the tubing is longer on side B; thus, more water is in the tubing on side B. This means that a greater weight of water is trying to pull the water clockwise than counterclockwise, so the water will flow clockwise, from the higher container to the lower container. The flow continues until the water level in container A drops below the end of the tube or until the two water levels are the same.

An analogy of a siphon is a chain draped over a smooth rod. If one end of the chain on the rod is longer than the other end, the long end falls and pulls the short end up and eventually over the rod.

The Family Science Challenge and classroom Science Activity 1 show that the liquid will not run out of the narrow-diameter tubing if one end is sealed. The air that is trapped above the water and the air outside the tubing work to keep the water in the tube. Gravity causes the water in the tube to be pulled down a very small amount, and then the water forms a droplet on the bottom of the tube. As this happens, the space in the tube that is occupied by the air becomes slightly larger. Since the gas particles are now moving around in a slightly larger space, they do not strike the surface of the liquid as often. Since the pressure exerted by a gas depends upon how often the gas particles strike a surface, the pressure inside the tube is slightly lower than the pressure outside the tube. This difference is just enough to allow the atmospheric pressure outside the tube to hold the water in the tube. When the top of the tube is opened again, the water falls out. The atmospheric pressure at the top of the tube is now equal to the atmospheric pressure at the bottom. This allows the force of gravity to take over and pull the water out of the tube.

When the tube is formed into a "U" shape with the ends uncovered, the water level is the same on both sides of the tube. This is because the water on each side is exposed to the same pull of gravity. When the shape is changed to a "J," water will come out the lower end if it is below the level of water in the higher end.

The overflow device in classroom Science Activity 2 is not a siphon. It is simply a tube that allows water to run in one end and out the other. Atmospheric pressure pushes on both ends of the tubing, so it is the additional pressure due to the liquid that forces it through the tubing.

The Tantalus Cup, on the other hand, is a siphon. Once the bent tubing is filled with water and a bit more is added to the funnel, the siphon starts working and does not stop until the end inside the funnel is out of the water.

Siphons have many practical applications, including the "goosenecks" found in plumbing fixtures. Look under a kitchen or bathroom sink and you will see a structure that looks like the "J" formed in Science Activity 1. Toilets contain similar structures. The siphon in a toilet prevents sewer gas from moving up and out through the toilet. (See Figure 2.)

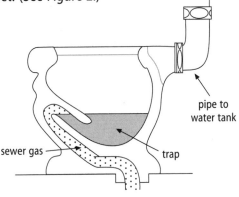

Figure 2

The siphon area of the toilet is full of water. When the toilet is flushed, water is added to one side and pushes the water through the siphon into the sewer pipes. When the water drains below the low point of the siphon, air fills the sewer line side of the siphon and the siphoning action stops. Repeated flushing or addition of water from a bucket repeats the siphoning behavior.

Cross-Curricular Integration

Home, Safety, and Career

- Visit a pet store and examine the siphons available to clean aquariums. Compare and contrast the technology involved in different siphon inventions. Compare prices and efficiency in moving water.
- Research the history of the modern toilet and its use of a siphon.
- What other devices use siphons? Have students research to find out.

Language Arts

- After performing the Science Activities and reading the Greek myth about Tantalus, write the word "tantalize" on the board. Ask students to speculate what it means. Then share the definition of the word with them.
- Have students write poems to describe what it would be like to be a drop of water moving through a siphon. They may want to write their poems in the shape of a siphon system or a water drop.

Social Studies

- Study the Greek myth about Tantalus, a favorite mortal of the gods until he betrayed them. They banished him and sentenced him to hang from a tree forever. Every time he tried to drink from a pond under the tree, it dried up. Every time he reached for the fruit hanging from the tree, the wind blew it away. Why was the tantalus cup given its name?
- Research the water systems that different civilizations invented to move water from place to place. For example, the Romans built aqueducts, and windmills were used in western America to pump water. Investigate uses of siphons in agriculture.
- Have students investigate how water moves in and out of their houses. You may want to ask a representative from the local water company to come and talk to your class.

Balance Bonanza

Enrich the **"Balancing Butterflies"** *activity in the book* Science Night Family Fun from A to Z *or use as a stand-alone lesson on balance and center of gravity.*

Students investigate how the center of gravity can be moved.

. . . . **Key Science Topics**

- balance
- center of gravity

. . . . **Average Time Required**

Setup	10	minutes
Performance	15–25	minutes
Cleanup	5	minutes

· · · · · · · · · · · · · · National Science Education Standards

Science as Inquiry Standards

- Abilities Necessary to Do Scientific Inquiry
  Students conduct simple experiments to determine the balance points of paper figures with and without added paper clips.

  Students use their observations to explain how a figure's balance point changes when paper clips are added to the figure.

  Students listen to and discuss the ideas and explanations of the other students.

  Students communicate their findings by writing answers to the questions and by participating in the Child/Adult Discussion.

Physical Science

- Properties of Objects and Materials
  Objects have mass and shape that affect their ability to be balanced.

- Position and Motion of Objects
  Objects have balance points, which may change when additional mass is added to the figure.

- Motion and Forces
  When another force (such as a gentle breeze) acts on a stably balanced object, gravity helps to pull that object back into its balanced position.

Science and Technology

- Abilities of Technological Design
  Students apply the knowledge gained in the Family Science Challenge to other objects.

  Students propose and implement solutions to the problem of how to balance the regularly shaped objects both horizontally and vertically.

  Students share their solutions through written and drawn answers to questions and through participation in the Follow-Up Discussion.

History and Nature of Science

- Science as a Human Endeavor
  Students learn that highwire and other balancing acts in a circus are based on principles of physics.

- History of Science
  Students research the contributions of scientists and engineers toward the construction and preservation of the Leaning Tower of Pisa.

Science Activity

Materials

cardstock square • paper clips

Challenge

Can you balance the square card on your finger?

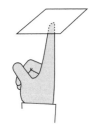

Figure 1

Procedure

❶ Try to balance the square card on the tip of your index finger. Once you get the square to balance, place the index finger from your other hand on the top of the square directly over your balance finger. (See Figure 1.) This will ensure that your square will not fall.

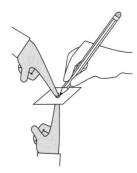

Figure 2

❷ Have your partner draw a circle around the spot where your index finger meets the square. Draw the location of the balance point on the square in Figure 2 and label this point "1."

❸ Place a paper clip on one corner of the square as shown in Figure 3.

? *Where is the balance point now? Find it and draw it on your square. Label this point "2."*

❹ Add a paper clip to another corner.

? *Is the balance point different?* _____

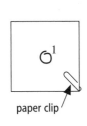

paper clip

Figure 3

❺ Design an experiment to find out if the balance point is affected by the number of paper clips you add and which corners you add them to.

? *What did you do? What did you learn?*

_____

_____

_____

6 Now try to balance the square on one of its edges on the tip of your index finger. Use as many paper clips as you need. If you need a hint, ask your teacher.

? *Draw the location of the paper clips you used on the figure below.*

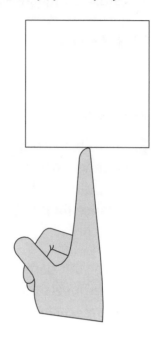

Teacher Notes for the Science Activity

Materials

Per class
* scissors

Per group
* cardstock
* paper clips

Setup

Cut card stock or index cards into squares approximately 2 inches x 2 inches.

Answers and Observations

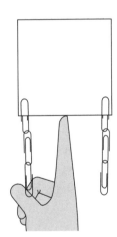

❸ *Where is the balance point now? Find it and draw it on your square.*

The balance spot should be in the middle of the square.

❹ *Is the balance point different?*

Yes. It has moved toward the paper clip.

❺ *What did you do? What did you learn?*

The balance spot may remain in the middle of the square (if equal numbers of paper clips are attached to each corner) or may move to a new position (if equal numbers of paper clips are not added to all corners).

❻ *Draw the location of the paper clips you used on the figure below.*

See Figure 1. (Important: For best results, the first paper clips should not be pushed all the way onto the paper square.)

Suggestions for Follow-Up

Have students share their observations with the class and discuss possible reasons for similarities and differences. Ask students to summarize how adding weight (paper clips) affects the balance spot of the square.

Assessment

Materials

Per class
- 4–5, 8½-inch x 11-inch sheets of cardstock
- pencil or pen
- scissors

Per group
- 2 different cardstock geometric figures
- paper clips
- scissors

Setup

Use the Geometric Shapes Template (provided) to trace different shapes (regular geometric shapes such as circle, triangle, hexagon, and pentagon) onto cardstock, and cut out the shapes. Make enough cardstock figures to provide groups with a selection of shapes.

Challenge

Have each group select one of the cardstock shapes. Challenge each group to use what they have learned to balance the shape any way they like and determine the balance point. Instruct students to draw the shape in the balance position (including any paper clips) and mark the balance point. Ask them to respond to this question: How do your results with this shape compare with your results with the square?

Have each group switch shapes with another group and repeat the challenge. Instruct students to draw the new shape in the balance position as they did before. Have groups who tried the same shape compare their results and discuss how they were similar and different. After this discussion, have students write one important fact or idea they learned in this lesson in their science journals.

Science Explanation

This section explains the science concepts in this lesson as well as in the "Balancing Butterflies" Family Science Challenge in Science Night Family Fun from A to Z. *It is intended for the teacher's information and may be modified as necessary for discussion with students.*

Objects usually can be balanced at or directly below their center of gravity, the point at which the weight of the object seems to be concentrated. (Center of gravity is sometimes called center of mass.) That is, the object behaves as if all of its weight were located at this point. In some cases (such as in a ring or doughnut shape), the center of gravity of an object may be where no actual material exists.

The butterflies in the Family Science Challenge and the squares and other shapes in the classroom Science Activity and the Assessment all have a center of gravity determined by their shape. All regular geometric shapes (which are shapes with equal side lengths and equal angles, as well as circles) and all uniform planar (flat) objects have the center of gravity in the geometric center because they are symmetrical. While the butterflies in the Family Science Challenge are irregularly shaped, they are flat, uniform objects, so you can determine the center of gravity by experimenting to find the balance point. It's interesting to note that finding the geometric center of the butterfly using mathematics would require calculus, but with physics you can do so by finding the balance point.

The center of gravity of an irregular object can be found without trial-and-error balancing. If you suspend an object from a single point, the center of gravity of the object will hang directly below or at the point of suspension. If an object is suspended from any number of points in succession and a vertical line is drawn through each support point, all lines will cross at the center of gravity.

Changing the mass of an object changes the center of gravity; adding paper clips to the butterflies or geometric shapes adds mass. Unless the mass is added equally and symmetrically (such as paper clips of equal mass placed on opposite corners of a square), the balance point of the system changes.

An object can actually balance with its center of gravity above or below the point of support (as well as at the point of support). However, if the center of gravity is above the support point, the object is very unstable. For example, with much practice and a lot of control, someone could balance the cardboard square on its edge without adding any paper clips. However, this is not very easy because if the square should tip even a small amount, gravity will pull it away from the balanced position. In contrast, if you balance an object in such a way that its center of gravity hangs below its point of support, the object is more stable. For example, adding a chain of paper clips to the corners of the square moves the center of gravity below the point where your finger supports the square's edge. Even when tipped a little, the square will not fall because gravity pulls it back into position.

Cross-Curricular Integration

Art and Music

- Have the students draw their own balanced figures. These figures could be circus performers or other people or animals that are good balancers.
- Have the students make a mobile. (See figure.) They can use hangers, plastic straws, pennies, and fishing line cut in various lengths. Have each student choose a theme for his/her mobile and collect objects or pictures to carry out the theme. Have them use fishing line to tie an object to the end of each straw and then hang the straws from the hanger or from each other with more fishing line. When the students are finished, have them tape pennies or washers on the objects to make them balance. (The hanger and the straws should be level.)

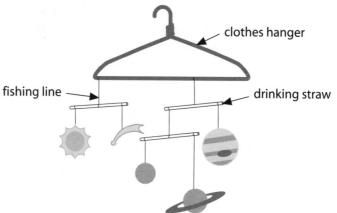

clothes hanger

fishing line

drinking straw

Language Arts

- After students have completed this activity, show them the cover of *Mirette on the High Wire,* by Emily Arnold McCully (Putnam, ISBN 0399221301). Ask, "What is Mirette doing? Why is she holding her arms out?" Read the book to the students. Ask them to look for pages that show balancing. After reading the story, you may wish to have the students design Mirette cutouts to balance on the tips of their fingers.
- Have the students write a cinquain poem about balancing objects. (In the lower grades, the cinquain can be written as a whole class activity. By third grade, most students can compose their own.) If the students do the first art integration, have them write their poems around the outline of their drawn figures. The standard form for a cinquain is as follows:

Noun
Adjective, adjective
Question
Four participles
Noun

- Read aloud or have students read one or more of the following books:
  - *Bearymore,* by Don Freeman (Puffin, ISBN 0-14-050-279-3)
    A bear learns to ride a unicycle on a tightrope.
  - *George and Martha,* by James Marshall (Houghton Mifflin, ISBN 0-395199727)
    Two lovable hippos teach the meaning of friendship in five separate vignettes.
  - *Gravity is a Mystery,* by Franklyn M. Branley (Harper & Row, ISBN 0-06-445057-0)
    Explains in simple text and illustrations what is known about the force of gravity
  - *Just a Little Bit,* by Ann Tompert (Houghton Mifflin, ISBN 0-395-77876X)
    Elephant and his friends try to ride a seesaw together.
  - *High-Wire Henry,* by Mary Calhoun and Erick Ingraham (Morrow, ISBN 0-688-08983-6)
    Henry the cat learns tightrope walking using a stick and his tail to maintain balance.
  - *The Napping House,* by Audrey Wood (Harcourt Brace Jovanovich, ISBN 0152567119)
    People and animals in a house balance on top of each other like a pyramid.
  - *Up, Down, and Around,* by Millicent Ellis Selsam (Doubleday, ISBN 0-385-09863-4)
    Explains the effects of gravity on human beings, satellites, the sun, moon, and planets.
  - *Which Way Is Up?,* by Gail Kay Haines (Atheneum, ISBN 0-385-09863-4)
    An explanation of gravity and the discoveries that have been made about it—although we still don't know exactly how it works.

Life Science

- Have the students study how we change the center of gravity of our bodies to remain balanced while walking, running, standing, or bending over.
- Discuss the use of crutches or prosthetic limbs to maintain balance and mobility.

Mathematics

- Study symmetry in shapes, including symmetry in nature.

Physical Education

- Have the students take turns walking on a balance beam. Then have them try walking on the beam while carrying a heavy weight in one hand.
- Use a seesaw to show balance.
- Have students stand with their heels against a wall. Have them carefully bend over and try to touch their toes.

Social Studies

- Have students study the history of balancing acts in the circus.
- Research the Leaning Tower of Pisa located in Pisa, Italy, and the efforts made by its original engineer and others in later centuries to keep it from falling.

Geometric Shapes
Template

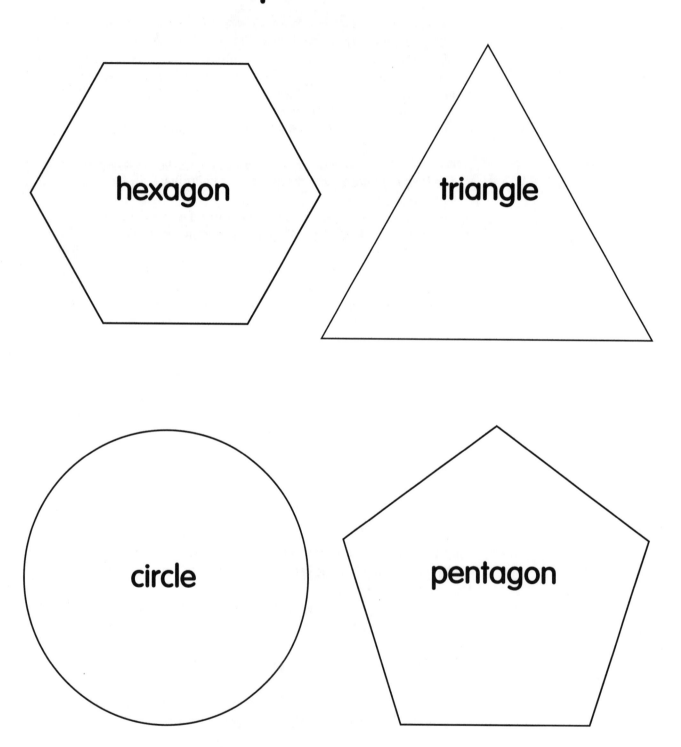

hexagon

triangle

circle

pentagon

Lesson C

Counterrevolution

*Enrich the **"Cool 'Copters"** activity in the book* Science Night Family Fun from A to Z *or use as a stand-alone lesson on gravity and air resistance.*

Students fold paper "whirligigs" and examine the effects of shape and mass on the way the whirligigs fall.

. . . . **Key Science Topics**

- air resistance
- gravity

. . . . **Average Time Required**

Setup   10 minutes
Performance   10 minutes
Cleanup   5 minutes

 **Overview**

. . . . ## National Science Education Standards

Science as Inquiry Standards

- Abilities Necessary to Do Scientific Inquiry
  Students conduct a simple investigation of the helicopter and make systematic observations of the effects that folding and adding paper clips have on the helicopter's flight.

  Students construct reasonable explanations of the effects that folding and adding paper clips have on the helicopter's flight.

Physical Science

- Position and Motion of Objects
  The motion of the helicopter can be described by its position, direction of motion, and speed.

  Objects with blades or wings tend to rotate as they fall.

  Unbalanced forces will cause changes in the speed, direction, and rotation of the helicopter's motion.

Science and Technology

- Abilities of Technological Design
  Students discuss the characteristics of a superior whirligig design.

  In the Assessment, students design and conduct a set of experiments to investigate variables that affect the flight of the helicopter.

  Students present their conclusions to their classmates.

Science Activity

Materials

several weights of paper • ruler • scissors • tape

Challenge

Can you create a whirligig that spins when you drop it?

Procedure

❶ Select one piece of paper, and use the ruler to carefully measure a six-inch square. Cut out the square. Hold up the paper square and drop it to the ground.

? *Describe how the paper falls.*

_____

_____

_____

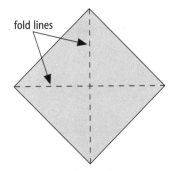

Figure 1

❷ Bring two opposite corners of the square together so it folds into a triangle. Unfold. Bring the other two corners together so the square folds into a triangle again. Unfold. The square should look like Figure 1.

❸ Fold the sides inward three times as shown in Figure 2. You will end up with a long thin piece of paper.

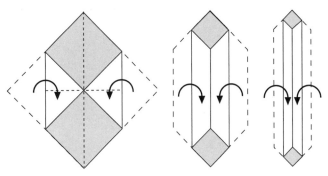

Figure 2

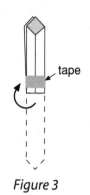

tape

Figure 3

❹ Fold the long thin piece of paper in half as shown in Figure 3. Tape it together about one inch from the bottom.

❺ Hold up the folded paper and drop it to the ground.

? *Does the folded paper fall differently than the unfolded paper?*

_____

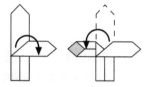

Figure 4

❻ Fold the paper as shown in Figure 4 to create two flaps.

❼ Drop the whirligig with the flaps facing up. If the whirligig does not rotate as it falls, try adjusting the flaps.

? *Does the whirligig with flaps fall differently than before? Explain.*

_____

_____

_____

❽ Try making several different whirligigs using different weights of paper. Test them as before.

? *What did you do? What did you find out?*

_____

_____

_____

Teacher Notes for the Science Activity

Materials

Per student or group
- several weights of paper (pieces at least 6 inches square), including
  - ordinary text-weight paper (such as photocopy paper)
  - gift-wrapping tissue paper
  - paper towel or napkin

 Do not use cardstock; it forms sharp corners that can be dangerous if the whirligigs are thrown.

- ruler
- scissors
- tape

Answers and Observations

❶ *Describe how the paper falls.*

The paper flutters to the ground, probably turning different ways as it falls.

❺ *Does the folded paper fall differently than the unfolded paper?*

The folded paper will usually fall straight to the ground.

❼ *Does the whirligig with flaps fall differently than before? Explain.*

The whirligig with flaps will usually fall more slowly and spin as it falls. It may start to spin and then tumble to the ground.

❽ *What did you do? What did you find out?*

The whirligig made of heavier paper may fall too fast to spin very much before it reaches the ground. The whirligig made of lighter paper will probably fall more slowly and may spin more as it falls. However, lighter whirligigs may tumble more.

Suggestions for Follow-Up

Try making other changes to the whirligig, such as adding weight with paper clips or changing the length of the flaps. (You may want to provide different sizes and types of paper clips to allow students to experiment further with mass and its effect on the whirligig. For example, two plastic paper clips will add less mass than two metal paper clips.) What did students do? What did they find out? As a class, write or discuss what makes a superior whirligig.

 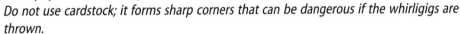

Assessment

Materials

Per student or group
- 3 helicopter patterns (template provided; each has a different shape)
- scissors
- paper clips

Setup

Photocopy the helicopter template (provided) onto regular white paper.

Challenge

Challenge students to design a set of experiments to investigate variables that may affect the descent of the helicopters. Explain that they have three different designs to test. If necessary, review the concept of designing a scientific experiment.

If students did not participate in the Family Science Challenge, they may have difficulty identifying possible variables without some help. If desired, have students do the following steps before designing their experiments:

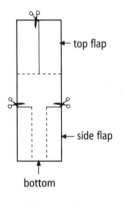

Figure 1

❶ Cut out helicopter X-1 on the heavy black lines and cut the thinner solid black lines to make the flaps, but do not fold any of the flaps. (See Figure 1.) Hold the helicopter above your head and drop it with the bottom pointing down.

❷ Fold in only the side flaps, and make sure the top flaps are both still unfolded as shown in Figure 2a. Hold the helicopter above your head and drop it with the bottom pointing down.

❸ Fold the top flaps opposite ways along the dotted line as indicated in Figure 2b. Hold the helicopter above your head once again and drop it as before.

❹ Place a paper clip on the helicopter at the bottom and try dropping it as before.

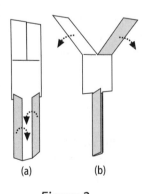

Figure 2

As a class, discuss some general ideas for designing the experiments, such as how (or whether) the helicopter is folded, whether weight is added (and if so, how much and where), how the helicopter is held when dropped, and the height from which it is dropped. Instruct students to write out their experiment plans, conduct the same tests with each of the three designs, and record their results. Give students an opportunity to present their conclusions to the class.

As a class, discuss any general conclusions that students can make based on everyone's results. After this discussion, have students write one important fact or idea they learned during this lesson in their science journals.

C 'Copter Patterns for Assessment

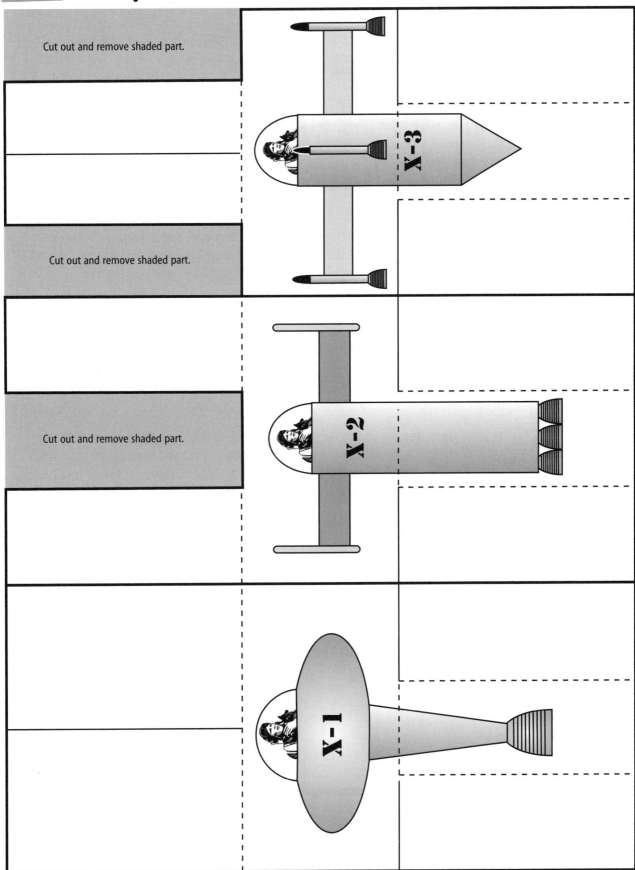

Cut out and remove shaded part.

Cut out and remove shaded part.

Cut out and remove shaded part.

X-3

X-2

X-1

Science Explanation

This section explains the science concepts in this lesson as well as in the "Cool 'Copters" Family Science Challenge in Science Night Family Fun from A to Z. *It is intended for the teacher's information and may be modified as necessary for discussion with students.*

When you let go of the whirligig or paper helicopter, two forces begin acting on it: gravity and air resistance. Gravity is the downward pull toward the surface of the Earth. Air resistance is an upward force that acts on the portion of an object's surface area that is parallel to the ground. This upward force partially cancels out the downward force of gravity.

When you drop a sheet of paper, it does not stay in any particular position. Air resistance acts over the whole surface of paper, and it flutters to the ground. When you drop the unfolded whirligig or helicopter, it behaves just like an ordinary piece of paper.

When you fold the whirligig paper into a thin shape without flaps or fold in the helicopter's side flaps (leaving the top flaps straight up), the extra thickness of paper concentrates the mass at the center part of the bottom. Now, when you drop the whirligig or helicopter (bottom pointing down), it often falls straight. Air resistance does not affect it much, since not much of the paper surface is parallel to the ground as it falls.

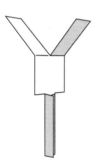

When you fold open the top flaps of the whirligig or helicopter, you create angled blades which the molecules in the air hit and bounce off at an angle. This causes two different things to happen to the helicopter: 1) it falls more slowly, and 2) it spins.

Adding a paper clip to the bottom of the whirligig or helicopter adds mass to the bottom, and this helps to stabilize the paper toys as they fall. However, adding too much mass will cause the toys to drop too fast and not allow them to spin.

To avoid confusion, you may want to point out to students that the paper helicopters are so named because as they fall, the folded flaps on top imitate the whirling blades of a real helicopter. However, make sure students realize that the blades of a real helicopter turn and lift the aircraft because its engines produce the power to do so.

Cross-Curricular Integration

Language Arts

- Read aloud or have students read the following book:
  - *Red Leaf, Yellow Leaf,* by Lois Ehlert (Harcourt, Brace, Jovanovich, ISBN 0152661972)
    This book traces the life cycle of sugar maple seeds, including how they spin as they fall to the ground.

Life Science

- Study seeds, such as maple seeds, that look like helicopter blades and are distributed by wind.

Mathematics

- Time the fall of a helicopter with no paper clips on the bottom. Add paper clips one at a time and drop the helicopter from the same height, timing each fall. Create a graph comparing the number of paper clips to the fall time.

Social Studies

- Have students trace the history of helicopters beginning with the sketches of Leonardo da Vinci (1452–1519).

Just for Fun

- Invite a helicopter pilot to speak to the class about how helicopters fly and the controls that are used in flying a helicopter.
- Take a field trip to an airport and observe helicopters.

Don't Be Dense

Enrich the "Disco Raisins" activity from the book Science Night Family Fun from A to Z *or use as a stand-alone lesson on buoyancy and gases.*

Students make raisins dance using baking soda and vinegar.

.... **Key Science Topics**

- buoyancy
- floating and sinking
- gases
- relative densities

.... **Average Time Required**

Setup	5 minutes
Performance	10–15 minutes
Cleanup	5 minutes

.... ## National Science Education Standards

Science as Inquiry Standards

- Abilities Necessary to Do Scientific Inquiry
Students predict what will happen when various solids are placed in water and in a carbonated soft drink in the Family Science Challenge.

Students conduct simple investigations to test their predictions, to develop cause-and-effect relationships using their observations, and to determine what happens when an acid reacts with carbonate or bicarbonate.

Students use their observations of the behavior of the raisins, popcorn kernels, and corks in the Family Science Challenge to explain this behavior.

Students develop cause-and-effect relationships using their observations of how water, vinegar, and baking soda react with each other.

Students discuss their predictions, observations, and conclusions with their adult partners and with their classmates.

Physical Science

- Properties of Objects and Materials
Raisins, popcorn kernels, and cork pieces like those used in the Family Science Challenge float or sink when placed in water because of their density relative to water.

The system made up of raisins plus gas bubbles floats in the Family Science Challenge because the very low density of the gas lowers the overall density of the system.

The gas in carbonated soft drinks such as those used in the Family Science Challenge can be separated from the liquid.

An acid reacts with carbonate or bicarbonate to form carbon dioxide and water.

- Position and Motion of Objects
Some objects in the Family Science Challenge alternate between floating and sinking in a cup of soft drink as their densities change over a period of time.

Science and Technology

- Abilities of Technological Design
Students use their observations to develop and implement solutions for inflating a balloon without touching it or blowing into it.

Students communicate and evaluate their solutions and classmates' solutions.

History and Nature of Science

- Science as a Human Endeavor
Students investigate how people have used their knowledge of density to create diving bells, submarines, and scuba gear.

Science Activity

Materials

raisins • scissors • water • clear plastic cup • straw • baking soda
• vinegar • ½-cup measure • 1-teaspoon measure

Challenge

Can you make raisins dance with the materials provided?

Procedure

Do not drink or eat any of the materials used in this activity. Do not share the straws.

❶ Use the scissors to carefully cut one raisin in half. (If the raisin is large, cut the halves in half.) Drop the raisin pieces into the plastic cup.

❷ Pour ½ cup water into the cup. Use a straw to blow bubbles in the water and see if you can get the raisins to rise to the surface.

? *Record your observations.*

_____

_____

_____

❸ Add 1 teaspoon baking soda to the water in the cup. Stir to mix.

? *What happens to the raisins?*

_____

_____

_____

❹ Pour 1 teaspoon vinegar into the mixture. Do you see any evidence that a chemical reaction is occurring?

? *What is happening in the mixture, and what is happening to the raisins?*

_____

_____

_____

❺ When the mixture settles down, add another teaspoon of vinegar.

? *Record your observations.*

_____

_____

_____

❻ Experiment to see whether you can get the raisins to dance by adding 1 more teaspoon water. How about 1 more teaspoon vinegar? 1 more teaspoon baking soda? Don't empty the cup or let it spill over.

? *Describe what you did and what you observed.*

_____

_____

_____

Teacher Notes for the Science Activity

Materials

Per class or per group
- raisins
- scissors
- water
- 10- or 12-ounce clear plastic cups
- straw
- baking soda
- white vinegar
- ½-cup measure
- 1-teaspoon measure

Answers and Observations

❷ *Record your observations.*

You can get the raisins to rise by blowing directly underneath them, but they will sink when the blowing stops.

❸ *What happens to the raisins?*

No change

❹ *What is happening in the mixture, and what is happening to the raisins?*

Bubbles occur in the mixture and on the surface of the raisins. The raisins rise to the surface, where the bubbles pop, causing the raisins to sink back to the bottom of the container.

❺ *Record your observations.*

Additional vinegar causes the reaction to begin again, and bubbles are again created.

❻ *Describe what you did and what you observed.*

Adding water causes no reaction. Adding vinegar creates a reaction only if all of the baking soda has not previously been used up. Adding baking soda produces bubbles if excess vinegar is still present in the mixture.

Suggestions for Follow-Up

Have students share and compare their experiment results. Ask students why they think the raisin halves behaved differently with the bubbles of carbon dioxide gas than they did with the bubbles of air from the straw.

Assessment

Materials

Per group
- balloon
- 1-L plastic soft-drink bottle
- baking soda
- vinegar
- water
- 1-teaspoon measure

Challenge

Challenge students to use the materials listed above and what they learned about the chemistry of baking soda, vinegar, and water to inflate a balloon without blowing into it and without touching it while it is being inflated. They may use any combination of chemicals they choose, but they must limit the quantities as follows:
- no more than 1 teaspoon baking soda
- no more than 3 teaspoons vinegar
- all the water they want

Emphasize that the balloon can contain liquid and/or solid; it doesn't have to contain only gas.

Allow groups time to design and test several methods. Instruct students to record their group's procedures and results in words and/or pictures in their science journals. When all groups have found a method that works, have them share their methods with the class. Compare the materials and amounts used by different groups. After the discussion, have students write one important fact or idea they learned during this lesson in their science journals.

Science Explanation

This section explains the science concepts in this lesson as well as in the "Disco Raisins" Family Science Challenge in Science Night Family Fun from A to Z. *It is intended for the teacher's information and may be modified as necessary for discussion with students.*

The Family Science Challenge illustrates the concept of relative density and how this is affected by the addition of gas bubbles. Objects that are less dense than a liquid will float in the liquid, while those that are more dense will sink in the liquid. Because many swimmers are more dense than water, they must exert energy to keep their heads above the water surface so they can breathe. Consequently, they may use a flotation device such as water wings or an inner tube to keep themselves afloat with their heads out of the water. These devices work by increasing the volume of the system (person plus flotation device) a lot while increasing the mass only a little. The flotation devices do this by trapping air (which has a relatively low density) inside. The large increase in the system's volume combined with the small increase in mass causes a net decrease in density. If this decrease makes the system sufficiently less dense than water, the flotation device will have done its job, and the person using the device will float. If the water wings or inner tube is deflated, the person will no longer float with his or her head above the water.

In the Family Science Challenge, the raisin pieces and popcorn kernels are more dense than the soft-drink solution and thus will sink in the soft drink. However, when the bubbles of carbon dioxide gas from the soft drink become attached to these solids, the bubbles give the combined solid-and-bubble system a lower density than that of the soft drink. That is, the bubbles (like the water wings) add a lot of volume to the system but very little mass. If enough bubbles are attached, the density of the combined system will be less than the density of the solution, and the bubble-covered raisin pieces and popcorn kernels will rise to the surface of the solution. At the surface, the gas bubbles "pop" and the carbon dioxide gas is lost into the air. The solids sink once again as a result of the loss of the gas bubbles. The process is repeated as long as sufficient carbon dioxide gas is available. Note that the size of the pieces is not a factor in their behavior. The only thing that matters is the density and how well the bubbles adhere to the object.

When the soft drink loses its carbonation, the raisin pieces and popcorn sink because bubbles of carbon dioxide are no longer available to increase the buoyancy of the solids. This observation indicates that the floating behavior is not a result of the relative densities of the soft-drink solution and the solids. In other words, "flat" soft-drink solution could be used as the control for the activity.

In the classroom Science Activity, the carbon dioxide gas is produced by the reaction of sodium bicarbonate (baking soda, $NaHCO_3$) solution and acetic acid ($HC_2H_3O_2$). (Vinegar is a 4–5% solution of acetic acid and water.) The reaction that occurs when the two solutions are mixed is shown below:

$$NaHCO_3(aq) \ + \ HC_2H_3O_2(aq) \longrightarrow CO_2(g) \ + \ H_2O\ (l) \ + \ NaC_2H_3O_2(aq)$$

sodium   acetic acid   carbon   water   sodium acetate
bicarbonate   dioxide

The amount of baking soda used in the activity is more than enough to react with the initial amount of vinegar added. Thus the reaction will continue if more vinegar is added and will produce additional carbon dioxide. Although some of the carbon dioxide that is produced through this reaction dissolves in the solution, most of it bubbles off as the gas visible during the reaction. These bubbles adhere to the solids, causing them to bob up to the surface as observed in the Family Science Challenge. The bubbles pop when they reach the surface, and the solid sinks to the bottom.

As more vinegar is added, less and less of the sodium bicarbonate remains available to react with it. The carbon dioxide bubbles eventually subside as the baking soda is used up, so the addition of vinegar has no further effect. When additional baking soda is added, bubbles are seen again because the baking soda in the solution reacts with the remaining vinegar that did not react in previous steps.

The initial step of blowing air through a straw does not cause the raisins to rise because large bubbles are formed in the straw and are forced out with considerable pressure. These large, fast-moving bubbles move quickly to the surface of the water and do not stick to the raisins. In contrast, the carbon dioxide bubbles are tiny and form slowly on the surface of the raisin, where they stick.

Cross-Curricular Integration

Art and Music

- Design an ad for a soft drink that contains raisins or other objects that "dance" when the bottle is opened. Include an explanation of how the dancing works.

Home, Safety, and Career

- Make a water-safety poster that includes information about flotation devices such as life jackets. Have students bring in water-safety devices and discuss as a class how and why the devices work.

Language Arts

- Read aloud or have students read the following book:
  - *Who Sank the Boat?* by Pamela Allen (Paper Star, ISBN 069811373X).
    A cow, a donkey, a sheep, a pig, and a mouse decide to go rowing in a very small boat. As more and more animals climb into the boat, the density of the system increases, until finally the mouse climbs in.
- Have students write and illustrate a story about using bubbles of gas to carry sunken treasures to the surface of the ocean.

Mathematics

- Measure the time the bobbing continues and the bobbing rates of raisins or unpopped popcorn kernels in different types of colorless or lightly colored soft drinks, including diet varieties.
- Use vermicelli instead of raisins in the soft drink. Break the pasta into different lengths and determine what effect, if any, the length of the pieces has on the rate of bobbing.

Social Studies

- Study the history and technology of diving bells, submarines, and scuba diving.

Just for Fun

- Have students make their own carbonated soda. Materials are available at many local shops and groceries. *Soda Science,* by Bernie Zubrowski (Beech Tree, ISBN 0688139833) is a Boston Children's Museum Book that offers ideas for designing and testing your own soda.

Lesson E

Evicting Air

Enrich the "Enlighten Yourself" activity in the book Science Night Family Fun from A to Z *or use as a stand-alone lesson on air pressure.*

Students use water of different temperatures to crush a plastic bottle.

Key Science Topics

- air pressure
- behavior of gases
- temperature

Average Time Required

Setup   5 minutes
Performance   10 minutes
Cleanup   5 minutes

· · · · · · · · · · · · · National Science Education Standards

Science as Inquiry

- Abilities Necessary to Do Scientific Inquiry
  Students observe temperature-related changes of gases and question what is happening.

  Students use careful, systematic observations of gases to develop explanations of gas behavior.

  Students record their observations and conclusions and discuss them with their adult partners, teacher, and classmates.

  Students think critically and logically to propose ways to return the crushed bottle to its original state.

Physical Science

- Properties and Changes of Properties in Matter
  A chemical reaction occurs as the candle burns.

  Gases expand when their temperature is increased and contract when their temperature is decreased.

  Materials can exist in different states—solid, liquid, and gas. Water can be changed from liquid to gas by heating, and from gas to liquid by cooling. Condensation of water vapor to a liquid state results in a large change in volume.

- Transfer of Energy
  The chemical energy stored in candle wax is converted to heat and light when the candle is burned.

Science Activity

Materials

2-L plastic soft-drink bottle with cap • hot tap water • sink or tub • tub of ice water

Challenge

Can you crush a plastic bottle with hot water?

Procedure

❶ Warm the outside of the uncapped bottle for a minute by pouring hot tap water over it in a sink or by submerging the bottle in a tub of hot tap water.

? *Is the air inside the bottle warmer or colder than the outside air?*

_____

_____

❷ Cap the bottle tightly, and remove it from the hot water. Place the bottle in a tub of ice water.

? *What happens to the temperature of the air inside the bottle?*

_____

_____

❸ As the bottle is cooling, watch and listen to the bottle.

? *What do you observe?*

_____

_____

❹ Suggest ways to return the bottle to its original shape without removing the cap.

_____

_____

_____

_____

❺ Try your ideas from step 4.

? *What do you observe?*

_____

_____

_____

_____

Teacher Notes for the Science Activity

Materials

Per student or group
- 2-L plastic soft-drink bottle with cap
- hot tap water

    While this activity works better when the water is hotter, be sure the tap water is not hot enough to burn skin. Water that is too hot may also cause the plastic bottle to shrink.

- sink or tub
- tub of ice water

Answers and Observations

❶ *Is air inside the bottle warmer or colder than the outside air?*

The air inside the bottle is warmed by the hot tap water and is warmer than the outside air.

❷ *What happens to the temperature of the air inside the bottle?*

The air inside gets colder.

❸ *What do you observe?*

As the bottle cools, it begins making popping noises and eventually collapses.

Suggestions for Follow-Up

Repeat the activity, but this time fill the bottle with hot water, swirl it around, empty it, and quickly cap the bottle tightly. Then place the bottle in the tub of ice water. Have students compare the results with their previous observations.

Assessment

Materials

Per class
- 2 aluminum soft-drink cans (clean and empty)
- hot plate

    You can use a votive candle or a Bunsen burner with ring stand and clamp as an alternative heat source, but a hot plate is recommended because all three cans can be heated at the same time. If you choose to use one of the alternatives, you'll need to modify the Procedure slightly.

- tongs, beaker tongs, or heat-resistant gloves
- 1 of the following wide-mouthed containers:
  - large clear bowl with sides at least 5 inches high
  - wide-mouthed jar (approximately 1-quart)
  - beaker (400- to 600-mL)
  - pie or cake pan
  - "pop beaker" made from a cut-off plastic 2-L soft-drink bottle
- ice water
- room-temperature water
- goggles

Per student
- Data Sheet (master provided)

Setup

Fill a wide-mouthed container three-quarters full of ice water.

Challenge

Explain to the students that during the demonstrations, you want them to clearly describe the procedure and the outcomes they observe. Their challenge will be to explain their observations.

Demonstration

❶ While students watch, pour about 5 mL water into a can. Place this can on the heated hot plate.

❷ Heat the can until the 5 mL water begins to boil. (This typically takes about 2–5 minutes to occur.) Do NOT allow the can to boil dry.

❸ Ask the students to predict what will happen when the can is lifted off the burner and inverted in cold water as shown in Figure 1. Once predictions are made, use a pair of tongs to carefully lift the can from the hot plate. In one motion, invert the can and submerge the open end in the ice water about an inch into the wide-mouthed container.

If you hold the tongs in your hand with your palm pointed up, inverting the can will be easier. Be sure to keep the opening of the can below the ice-water level until the can is crushed. A loud bang often accompanies the crushing of the can.

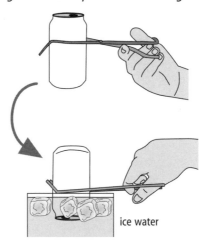

ice water

In one motion, invert the can and submerge the open end in ice water.

❹ Once the can is crushed, and with the students watching, lift the can straight out above the water to show that water drains out of the can. Ask the students where the water came from. (You may need to remind the students that this is the can that you poured about 5 mL water into initially.) *Much of the water that drained from the can was pushed into the can by the difference in pressure between the atmosphere and the inside of the inverted can. When the inverted can is cooled by the ice water, the pressure inside the can is reduced as the steam condenses to liquid water.*

Extending the Lesson

To reinforce the importance of the phase change in the demonstration above, you may also wish to repeat the demonstration with a can that is empty (except for air). To do this, heat a clean, empty aluminum can on a hot plate for 4–5 minutes. Ask students to predict what will happen when the heated can is lifted off the burner and inverted in cold water. Once predictions are made, use a pair of tongs to carefully lift the can from the hot plate. In one motion, invert the can and cover the open end in the ice water about an inch into the wide-mouthed container.

After about 5 seconds, and with the students watching, lift the can straight out above the water to show that water drains out of the can. Ask the students where the water came from.

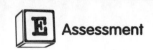

Challenge the students to explain the fact that some water drains from the can when it is lifted. *The can is primarily filled with hot air. While the hot air is cooled, only a small volume change occurs, so the pressure difference between the inside of the can and the atmosphere isn't enough to crush the can. However, some water is pushed into the can due to the reduction in pressure associated with the decrease in temperature when the hot air is cooled by the ice water.*

To help students form a clear understanding of the cause-and-effect relationship in these demonstrations, you may want to create a class chart in which students contribute their observations.

Suggestions for Follow-Up

Have students propose explanations for the behavior of each can using evidence from the class chart. Give students a chance to listen to and consider the explanations proposed by other students. They should remain open to and acknowledge different ideas and be able to accept the skepticism of others. Lead them in a discussion of the effect that a phase change has on the volume of the material. Give students a chance to revise their explanations. Discuss as a class.

Science Explanation

This section explains the science concepts in this lesson as well as in the "Enlighten Yourself" Family Science Challenge in Science Night Family Fun from A to Z. *It is intended for the teacher's information and may be modified as necessary for discussion with students.*

In the Family Science Challenge, a jar is placed over a lit candle that sits in a pan of water. As the jar is lowered over the candle, the air in the jar is heated. Heating a gas causes its volume to increase. Because the jar is open at the mouth, much of the gas originally in the jar is pushed out. This escaping air can at times be seen as bubbles at the point when the mouth of the jar is pushed beneath the water's surface, but these bubbles do not last for long.

After the water seals the mouth of the jar, the water level begins to rise inside the inverted bottle, the candle goes out, and the water continues to rise. To understand what causes these latter observations, it is useful to first consider what happens when the candle burns. The chemical reaction that occurs when a candle burns is shown by the following equation:

$$2\ C_{20}H_{42}\ (g)\ +\ 61\ O_2\ (g)\ \rightarrow\ 40\ CO_2\ (g)\ +\ 42\ H_2O\ (g)$$

| candle wax | oxygen gas | carbon dioxide gas | water vapor gas |

In the reaction, candle wax reacts with oxygen to produce carbon dioxide gas and water vapor. The flame goes out as the amount of oxygen falls below that needed to sustain combustion. (While oxygen is consumed in the combustion of candle wax, oxygen still remains in the bottle even after the flame goes out.)

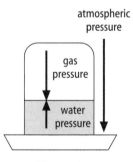

atmospheric pressure

gas pressure

water pressure

Figure 1

The water movement up the neck of the bottle does not result from the consumption of oxygen, but rather from the lowering of the pressure inside the container, which is caused by two factors. The first and most important factor is that the water produced in the combustion reaction is initially in the gaseous state, but it quickly cools below 100°C, and as a result, much of it condenses to the liquid state. Because liquid water occupies much, much less space than gaseous water, the gaseous volume inside the jar decreases rather dramatically. A secondary (and less influential) factor is that the pressure inside the container decreases as the gases cool after the flame goes out. Because the atmospheric pressure outside the jar is greater than the air pressure inside the jar, water is pushed into the jar. (See Figure 1.) The water movement ceases when the atmospheric pressure equals the sum of the gas pressure inside plus the pressure exerted by the column of water inside the jar, as shown in the following equation.

pressure outside = pressure inside

atmospheric pressure = gas pressure + pressure exerted by water column
(outside jar)   (inside jar)   (inside jar)

In the classroom Science Activity, heating the 2-L bottle with hot water warms the gas inside, which increases its kinetic energy. This increased energy of motion causes the amount of empty space between the gas molecules to increase. This pushes some of the gas molecules out of the mouth of the bottle. When the bottle is capped and cooled, the amount of empty space between the gas molecules returns to what it had been originally. This amounts to a decrease in the volume of the trapped air in the bottle. Because the sides of the bottle are flexible, it is then crushed by the atmospheric pressure. This crushing can be reversed by reheating the bottle and allowing air inside to increase in temperature, which causes an increase in pressure.

In the Assessment, a can is also crushed by differences in pressure when it contains a small amount of steam, but it holds its form when it contains only hot air.

References

Birk, J.P. "The Persistence of The Candle-and-Cylinder Misconception," *Journal of Chemical Education.* July, 1999, *76* (7), 914–916.

"Investigating a Burning Candle"; *Fun with Chemistry: A Guidebook of K–12 Activities;* Sarquis, M., Sarquis, J., Eds.; Institute for Chemical Education: Madison, WI, 1993; Vol. 2, pp 339–346.

Cross-Curricular Integration

Art

- Make a flip book of the Family Science Challenge that shows the water rising in the jar and the behavior of the candle flame.

Earth Science

- Research how changes in air pressure affect weather.
- Investigate how differences in temperature and air pressure relate to the development of thunderstorms and tornados.
- Have a meteorologist visit the classroom and include a discussion of pressure changes in a talk about weather.
- Look at different weather instruments that measure air pressure and see how they work.
- Discuss how and why some airplanes are pressurized.

Language Arts

- Read aloud or have students read one or more of the following books:
  - *Hot-Air Henry,* by Mary Calhoun (Mulberry, ISBN 0-688-04068-3)
    A Siamese cat stows away on a hot-air balloon and ends up taking a fur-raising flight across the mountains.
  - *Weather Words and What They Mean*, by Gail Gibbons (Holiday House, ISBN 0823408051)
    Simple sentences and cheerful illustrations introduce weather concepts.
  - *National Audubon Society's First Field Guide—Weather* (Scholastic, ISBN 0590054880)
    This guide gives detailed information and background including an identification guide to help students begin to recognize and understand weather patterns.

Life Science

- Investigate how people are affected by changes in air pressure. Some doctors believe that people's moods as well as their physical condition can be affected by air pressure changes.

Mathematics

- Use a stopwatch to measure the time (in seconds) it takes for the candle in the Family Science Challenge to go out. Average the results.
- Look up local air pressure readings in the newspaper for a week and graph the results.

Social Studies

- Research the history of hot-air balloons.
- Look through *The Old Farmer's Almanac* for weather signs and clues about changing weather patterns and how they relate to changes in air pressure.

Learn how people used to foretell weather based on things they could observe in nature.

- Look for high-altitude baking instructions on cake mixes. How does this relate to air pressure?

Just for Fun

- Attach a paper-cup gondola to a slightly underinflated helium balloon. Heat up the balloon with a hair dryer. Have helium balloon races or contests to see how much balloons can carry in their gondolas.
- If a student is going on a trip in an airplane, have him or her take along a plastic bottle and cap it at a high altitude. Have the student leave the cap on and observe what happens to the bottle after the plane lands.

Floppy Flatworms

Enrich the **"Frisky Fish"** *activity in the book* Science Night Family Fun from A to Z, *or use as a stand-alone lesson on absorption and capillary action.*

Students explore absorption and capillary action by making wiggly worms.

Key Science Topics

- absorption
- capillary action
- evaporation

Average Time Required

Setup	5	minutes
Performance	5–10	minutes
Cleanup	5	minutes

.... National Science Education Standards

Science as Inquiry Standards

- Abilities Necessary to Do Scientific Inquiry
  Students speculate about what causes the movement of the cellophane fish in the Family Science Challenge.

  Students conduct simple investigations to determine what causes the movement of the cellophane fish in the Family Science Challenge.

  Students conduct an investigation to determine the effects of water on a straw-wrapper "worm."

  Students design and conduct an investigation to determine the effects of using various types of paper for an unfolding paper flower.

  Students develop an explanation based on the results of their tests.

  Students use their observations of different types of paper to develop cause-and-effect relationships about why the folded paper flowers reacted as they did when water was added.

  Students discuss the causes of the behavior of the cellophane fish with their adult partners in the Family Science Challenge.

  Students share their explanations for the behavior of the different paper flowers and listen to and analyze their classmates' explanations.

Physical Science

- Properties of Objects and Materials
  The frisky fish in the Family Science Challenge are made from a hygroscopic cellophane. Water moves through this cellophane by capillary action.

  Different types of paper are made with different materials that affect how the paper reacts to water.

  Water changes from the liquid to the gas state when heated. This process is called evaporation.

- Light, Heat, Electricity, and Magnetism
  Heat moves from the hand to the cellophane fish in the Family Science Challenge by conduction.

- Transfer of Energy
  Heat moves predictably in the Family Science Challenge from the warmer hand to the cooler fish until both reach the same temperature.

Science Activity

Materials

drinking straws with paper wrapping intact • strip of graph paper • zipper-type plastic bag • coffee stirrer • marker or crayon • small cup of water • dropper

Challenge

Can you make a wiggly worm using absorption and capillary action?

Procedure

❶ Place the strip of graph paper in a zipper-type plastic bag and seal the bag.

❷ Hold your wrapped straw upright, with one end on the desk or table. Grasp the paper covering at the top of the straw and push the paper firmly down to the bottom of the straw. Carefully pull out the straw from the paper "worm."

❸ Insert a coffee stirrer into the paper worm without stretching it.

❹ Determine how many squares long your paper worm is by laying the worm on the start line of the graph paper in the zipper-type plastic bag and counting the number of squares it covers. Color in this number of squares in the Observation Chart.

? *How many squares long is the worm?* _____

? *What do you think will happen when a drop of water is placed on the worm?*

_____

_____

❺ Be sure your paper worm is still on the start line of the graph paper. Use a dropper to place a drop of water on the worm.

Observation Chart			

| Dry Worm | After 1 drop of water | After 2 drops of water | After 3 drops of water |

? *What happens?*

_____

_____

_____

6 Determine how long your worm is now. Count the number of squares and color in this number of squares in the Observation Chart.

7 Add a second drop of water to the worm and record how long it is.

8 Add a third drop of water to the worm and record how long it is.

Teacher Notes for the Science Activity

Materials

Per class
• scissors

Per student
• drinking straws with paper wrapping intact
• Graph Paper Strip (master provided)
• zipper-type plastic bag
• coffee stirrer
• marker or crayon
• small cup about ¼ filled with water
• dropper

Setup

Photocopy the Graph Paper Strips master (provided) and cut apart the strips.

Answers and Observations

❺ *What happens?*

The worm wiggles and stretches out in the area where the water was added.

Reference

Sarquis, M.; Sarquis, J.; Williams, J. "Magic Worms," *Teaching Chemistry with TOYS;* McGraw-Hill: New York, 1995; pp 75–80.

Suggestions for Follow-Up

Have students share their observations, and discuss similarities and differences. Then have them write one important fact or idea they learned in this investigation in their science journals.

Assessment

Materials

Per class
- 3½-inch x 3½-inch piece of newsprint
- dropper
- small cup one-quarter filled with water

Per student
- flower pattern (master provided)
- 3½-inch x 3½-inch piece of newsprint
- 3½-inch x 3½-inch pieces of several different kinds of paper, such as facial tissue, copy paper, construction paper, and paper towels
- pencil
- scissors
- dropper
- small cup one-quarter filled with water

Setup

- Photocopy the flower patterns and cut them out for students to trace.
- Place a flower pattern on a piece of newsprint and trace around the pattern with a pencil.
- Cut out the flower you have traced onto the newsprint.

Demonstration

Before explaining the challenge to the students, demonstrate the following procedure to the class.

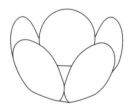

❶ Using a newsprint flower prepared in Setup, loosely fold all of the flower's petals in toward the center as shown in the figure at left.

❷ Use the dropper to drop water in the center of the flower, 1–2 drops at a time. The petals should unfold.

Challenge

Challenge students to design an experiment to determine how different types of paper respond in this activity. The students should follow the procedure you demonstrated for them when they are testing the different papers.

Have students keep careful notes and observations of their procedures and the results. Ask students to make observations about the paper before and after it is wet. When all students are finished, have them share their results with the class. Lead a discussion that encourages students to compare their results with those obtained by the rest of the class. Ask students, "Why do you think each type of paper behaved differently? What might have caused these differences?" Have on hand full, dry sheets of each type of paper tested so students can examine the texture of the paper again, if necessary. After the discussion, have students write one important fact or idea they learned from this lesson in their science journals.

Sample Results

Most of the papers need more water to make them unfold than the newsprint in the Demonstration did, and some may not unfold at all. Typical results are listed below.

- facial tissue—very little unfolding movement

- copy paper—unfolds with more water

- construction paper—unfolds with more water

- paper towel—little unfolding movement

Science Explanation

This section explains the science concepts in this lesson as well as in the "Frisky Fish" Family Science Challenge in Science Night Family Fun from A to Z. *It is intended for the teacher's information and may be modified as necessary for discussion with students.*

In the Family Science Challenge, the frisky fish is made from hygroscopic cellophane. "Hygro" means "water," and "scopic" means "to view or to find." The fish curls, twists, and bends in your hand because the cellophane absorbs moisture from your hand. The cellophane has tiny holes, or capillaries, through which the water moves into the cellophane. As the side of the fish toward your hand absorbs moisture, the cellophane begins to swell (like a flattened sponge swells when it gets wet). This causes the ends of the cellophane fish to curl up away from your hand. The heat of your hand causes the water to evaporate, creating air currents. The lightness of the cellophane makes it very susceptible to air currents, which adds to the "dancing" effect.

This type of movement does not occur when the cellophane fish is inside or on top of the plastic package. The plastic acts as a barrier that prevents the absorption of water from your palm by the cellophane. As a result, the cellophane fish does not move.

In the classroom Science Activity, water comes in contact with paper, a porous surface, and is absorbed (soaked up) into the pores of the material. The water moves throughout the material by capillary action caused by the attractive force between the water molecules and the molecules in the paper. As the paper absorbs the water, the paper swells, stretches out, and moves. This is what happens to both the paper worm in the Science Activity, causing it to wiggle and lengthen, and the paper flower in the Assessment, causing it to unfold.

Cross-Curricular Integration

Art

- Repeat the Assessment using a drop of food color instead of plain water. Try using different colors to see whether they behave the same way. Make a collage of your results.

Language Arts

- Read aloud or have students read the following book:
  - *Inch by Inch,* by Leo Leonni (Mulberry, ISBN 0688132839).
    A winsome, winning inchworm, proud of his ability to measure anything under the sun, finds out that his skill is also a lifesaver when a hungry bird gets a little too close.

Life Science

- Explore the nature of sweat glands and their location in the body.
- Use celery in colored water to show how water moves up plant stems to the leaves. Pick a piece of celery with leaves, cut off a stalk with a sharp knife, and immediately place it in undiluted liquid food color (red works well). Have students predict and then observe how the color moves by observing the changes in the celery. The amount of time this process takes depends on the length of the celery stick—allow about ½ hour for a 6-inch piece. You can break the celery stalk open to allow the food coloring inside the xylem and the phloem to be more visible. Try doing the activity with a white carnation; be sure to cut the stem immediately before you place it in the food color.
- Research sponge organisms and how they use flowing water and currents in the ocean to gather food and nutrients.

Mathematics

- Using different brands of paper towels cut into equal-sized strips, dip one end into water and measure how far the water has traveled up each strip after 1, 2, and 5 minutes.

Graph Paper Strips for the Science Activity

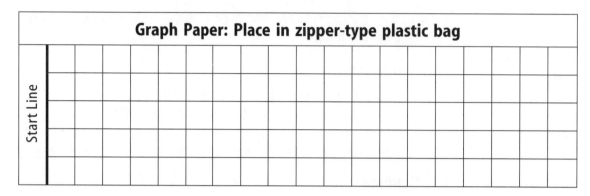

Graph Paper: Place in zipper-type plastic bag

Start Line

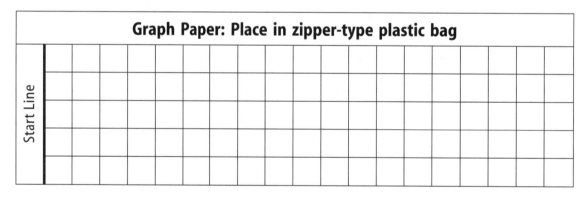

Graph Paper: Place in zipper-type plastic bag

Start Line

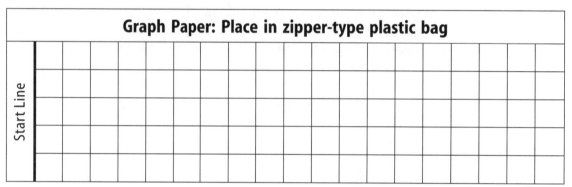

Graph Paper: Place in zipper-type plastic bag

Start Line

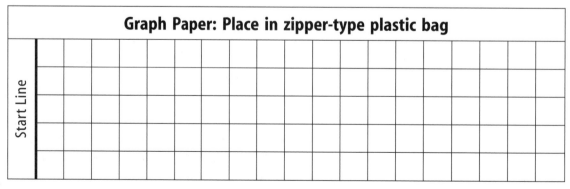

Graph Paper: Place in zipper-type plastic bag

Start Line

Flower Patterns for the Assessment

Gooey Globs

Enrich the **"Gobs of Fun"** activity in the book Science Night Family Fun from A to Z, *or use as a stand-alone lesson on polymers and viscosity.*

Students make three different putty recipes and compare their properties. In the demonstration, students build human polymer chains to show how cross-linkers work.

. . . . **Key Science Topics**

- cross-linkers
- physical properties
- polymers
- viscosity

. . . . **Average Time Required**

Science Activity

Setup	10 minutes
Performance	15–30 minutes
Cleanup	5–10 minutes

Classroom Demonstration

Performance	10 minutes

National Science Education Standards

Science as Inquiry Standards

- Abilities Necessary to Do Scientific Inquiry

  Students perform simple investigations with Gluep and glue putties to determine their properties.

  Students develop cause-and-effect relationships about how different recipes of Gluep and glue putty behave and what their ingredients are.

  Students and their adult partners analyze their results in terms of solid and liquid properties of Gluep during the Family Science Challenge.

  Students share their observations with their adult partners and with their classmates.

Physical Science

- Properties of Objects and Materials

  Gluep and glue putties have many observable properties.

  Materials can exist in different states—solid, liquid, and gas. Some materials like Gluep (called non-Newtonian fluids) have properties of both solids and liquids at the same time.

  The properties of mixtures (such as Gluep and glue putties) may vary with the types and amounts of the substances added to the mixture.

Science and Technology

- Abilities of Technological Design

  Students select a recipe of Gluep to "market" as a product by considering how it will be used by consumers and the properties each recipe of Gluep has.

  Students develop and implement a marketing plan for their Gluep while taking into account factors such as cost, production, and packaging.

  Students share their marketing plans with their classmates and students from other classes.

Science Activity

Materials

zipper-type plastic bags • adhesive labels or tape • permanent marker or pen • measuring spoons • 4 labeled cups of putty ingredients • water-soluble marker • index card or plastic bag • goggles

Challenge

Make different putty recipes and determine how various additives affect the final product.

Procedure

Wear goggles when measuring or adding borax solution. If you do not have goggles, your teacher will measure and pour the borax solution for you.

Part 1: Basic Putty

❶ Stick label or pieces of tape on three zipper-type plastic bags and use a pen or permanent marker to label them "basic putty," "talcum powder," and "lotion."

❷ Measure 2 tablespoons glue-water mixture and pour into the "basic putty" bag.

❸ Measure 2 teaspoons borax solution and pour into the "basic putty" bag with the glue-water mixture.

❹ Zip the bag closed and squeeze the bag gently to mix the contents. Continue mixing until a gel-like mass forms.

Part 2: Talcum Powder Additive

❶ Measure 1 teaspoon talcum powder and pour into the "talcum powder" bag.

❷ Measure 3 tablespoons glue/water mixture and add to the talcum powder in the bag.

❸ Measure 1 teaspoon borax solution and add to the mixture in the bag.

❹ Zip the bag closed and squeeze the bag gently to mix the contents. Continue mixing until a gel-like mass forms.

Part 3: Talcum Powder and Moisturizing Lotion

❶ Measure 1 teaspoon talcum powder and pour into the "lotion" bag.

❷ Measure 2 teaspoons oil-free moisturizing lotion and 4 teaspoons glue/water mixture and add these to the powder in the bag. Mix thoroughly.

❸ Measure 1 teaspoon borax solution into the bag.

❹ Zip the bag closed and squeeze the bag gently to mix the contents. Continue mixing until a gel-like mass forms.

Experimenting with the Putties

❶ Use your fingers to remove each putty from its bag. Some of the putties may be sticky at first, but they will become less sticky with handling.

❷ Experiment with each of the putties by squeezing it; by forming it into a ball and throwing it on a tile or linoleum floor; by pulling it gently and then quickly; and by pressing the putty on top of your name written with a water-soluble, felt-tipped marker on an index card or plastic bag. Record your observations.

❸ Let some of each putty dry out for several days. Observe the changes that have occurred. After each is dried out, try to get it to absorb some water.

❹ Store any remaining putties in their plastic bags. If any of the putties have begun to dry (other than the samples for step 3), mix in a small amount of water before storing them.

Teacher Notes for the Science Activity

Materials

Per group
- 3 zipper-type plastic sandwich bags
- 3 labels
- permanent marker or pen
- measuring teaspoon and tablespoon
- putty ingredients in small, labeled cups, as listed below
  - ½ cup 50/50 white glue/water mixture
  - 4 teaspoons saturated borax solution
  - 2 teaspoons talcum powder
  - 2 teaspoons oil-free moisturizing lotion such as Revlon® Clean and Clear®
- water-soluble marker
- index card or plastic bag
- goggles

Resources

Borax is available in the laundry section of grocery stores.

Safety

Wear safety goggles when preparing the borax solution. Have students wear goggles when measuring or pouring the borax solution. If you do not have student goggles, then we suggest that the teacher dispenses the borax solution.

Some people have developed an allergic reaction to dry, powdered borax. As a result, care should be taken when handling it. Avoid inhaling and ingesting borax. Use adequate ventilation in preparing the borax solution, and wash your hands after contact with the solid.

There is typically no danger in handling the glue putty, but you should wash your hands after use. Persons with especially sensitive skin or persons who know they are allergic to borax or detergent products should determine their sensitivity to glue putty by touching a small amount. Should redness or itching occur, wash the area with a mild soap and avoid further contact.

If glue putty spills on the carpet, apply vinegar to the spot and follow with a soap-and-water rinse. Do not let the glue putty harden on the carpet. Do not place glue putty on natural wood furniture; it will leave a water mark.

Setup

- Prepare the saturated borax solution in a 2-L plastic soft-drink bottle by adding ¼ cup borax to 1 quart warm water. Stir or shake to dissolve. Any undissolved solid can be left in the container. Label the bottle. The borax solution can be stored for several months. Shake the bottle well before use if the solution has been stored for long periods of time.

- Prepare the glue-water mixture by half-filling a 1-L plastic soft-drink bottle with glue and then adding water until the bottle is almost full. Shake well to mix. Label the bottle.

Disposal

The borax and glue solutions can be stored in closed containers for several months. Shake the bottles well before use if the solutions have been stored for long periods of time, and check the glue-water solution for signs of mold. Discard it if it is moldy.

Classroom Demonstration

❶ Ask for five volunteers to help you build a small section of a human polymer chain. Tell the class that each volunteer represents a monomer, one unit.

❷ Have monomers link arms or hold hands. (See Figure 1.) Each link represents a chemical bond. The chain they form is a simulation of a small section of a polymer chain that could have thousands of repeating units in it.

Figure 1

❸ Show the class how flexible the polymer chain is by leading the chain around the room, weaving between the students' desks or chairs. Ask this chain to remain standing.

❹ Ask five additional volunteers to come to the front of the class and form a new, separate polymer chain.

❺ Have the chains move around as before. Note that the movement of one chain does not depend on the movement of the other unless the chains get very close to each other.

❻ Designate one or two other volunteers to play the role of cross-linkers, which link the two polymer chains by holding onto both chains at once. (See Figure 2.)

cross-linkers

Figure 2

❼ The movement of one chain now depends on the movement of the other; the cross-linkers hold the chains together. Show this by having the chains try to move in the same direction. The cross-linkers will need to move also.

❽ Now have the chains move in opposite directions. The cross-link bond must break from one of the chains. If the chains are moved back together, the cross-links can reform in new places or in the same place.

Suggestion for Follow-Up

Have the class compare the properties of the basic putty to the properties of the putties with additives. Encourage students to discuss how each additive affected the properties of the putty. As a class, discuss which recipes make the best and worst putties.

References

Casassa, E.Z., Sarquis, M., and Van Dyke, C.H. "The Gelation of Polyvinyl Alcohol with Borax," *Journal of Chemical Education, 63*, 1986, pp 57–60.

"Glue Polymer"; *Chain Gang—The Chemistry of Polymers;* Sarquis, M., Ed.; Science in Our World Series; Terrific Science: Middletown, OH, 1995; pp 103–109.

"Gluep"; *Fun With Chemistry: A Guidebook of K–12 Activities;* Sarquis, M., Sarquis, J., Eds.; Institute for Chemical Education: Madison, WI, 1993; Vol. 2, pp 81–88.

Sarquis, M. "A Dramatization of Polymeric Bonding Using Slime," *Journal of Chemical Education, 63*, 1986, pp 60–61.

Sarquis, M. "Gluep," *Exploring Matter with TOYS: Using and Understanding the Senses;* McGraw-Hill: New York, 1997; pp 73–74.

Woodward, L. *Polymers All Around You;* Terrific Science: Middletown, OH, 1992.

Assessment

Materials

Per team of three students
- 6 teaspoons saturated borax solution
- 3 tablespoons white glue
- 3 tablespoons water
- measuring teaspoon and tablespoon
- red, green, and blue food colors
- zipper-top sandwich bags

Per student
- goggles

Safety

Wear safety goggles when preparing the borax solution. If you do not have student goggles, then we suggest that the teacher dispenses the borax solution.

Setup

Prepare the saturated borax solution as you did for the Science Activity.

Challenge

Give students a copy of the recipes in the following table and challenge them to predict the properties of the resulting glue putties. Have students prepare each of the recipes and record their observations. Ask students to propose explanations for the similarities and differences in the putties in terms of polymers and cross-linkers. Have them write one important fact or idea they learned during this lesson in their science journals.

Gluep Recipes	
Color of Gluep	Ingredients
red	1 tablespoon (15 mL) white glue no water 2 teaspoons (10 mL) borax solution 2 drops red food color
green	1 tablespoon (15 mL) white glue 1 tablespoon (15 mL) water 2 teaspoons (10 mL) borax solution 2 drops green food color
blue	1 tablespoon (15 mL) white glue 2 tablespoons (30 mL) water 2 teaspoons (10 mL) borax solution 2 drops blue food color

Science Explanation

> *This section explains the science concepts in this lesson as well as in the "Gobs of Fun" Family Science Challenge in* Science Night Family Fun from A to Z. *It is intended for the teacher's information and may be modified as necessary for discussion with students.*

Gluep (made in the Family Science Challenge) and other glue putties (made in the classroom Science Activity) are examples of cross-linked polymers. They are made from white glue (which contain the polymer polyvinyl acetate, PVAc) and borax, which is the active cross-linking agent. A polymer is a huge, chain-like molecule made by combining hundreds and thousands of small molecules called monomers. In fact, the word polymer comes from the Greek words "poly," meaning "many," and "mer," meaning "unit." The repeating unit in the PVAc polymer molecules is shown in the figure below.

To make the putties, a solution of borax is added to the polymer solution. When borax dissolves in water, some borate ions $\{B(OH)_4^-\}$ form. The borate ions form bridges, or cross-links, between the polymer chains, thereby connecting them to one another. (Review the demonstration.) These cross-links form in all three dimensions between the polymer chains and the borate ions. The resulting gel has a large amount of water trapped in this three-dimensional network. Using different amounts of water (as done in the Assessment) results in gels with different proportions of trapped water and thus different physical properties. For example, the blue gluep contains the most water and is the runniest. The red gluep contains the least water and is the most like a solid.

The putties belong to a class of materials that have properties of both a solid and a liquid. These materials are called non-Newtonian fluids. A low stress, such as slow pulling, allows them to flow, stretch, and even form a thin film. A high stress, such as a sharp pull, will cause the putty to break. Hitting a piece of putty with a light hammer will not cause splashing or splattering. Glue putties will also bounce to a small extent. These properties are due to the cross-linking described above.

The addition of talcum powder and lotion in the classroom Science Activity causes the formation of a semisolid compounded polymer with properties different from those of the three original components. The addition of the talcum powder creates additional cross-link sites and acts as a filler. The lotion acts as a slip agent and enhances the product's fluidity.

Cross-Curricular Integration

Art and Music

- Have students design packaging and advertisements for their choice of putties.

Language Arts

- Read aloud or have students read the following book:
  - *Horrible Harry and The Green Slime*, by Suzy Kline (Scholastic, ISBN 059043943X).

    Harry leads a mission to place cobwebs all over school, shows the class how to make green slime, and stages a "deadly skit" that has everyone on the edge of their seats.

Mathematics

- Determine how much it costs to make each type of putty in the Science Activity. Convert this to price-per-ounce cost for the finished putty. Have students check pricing and sizes of commercially available putty-type products and convert these to price-per-ounce costs. Graph these price-per-ounce costs on a chart. Ask students why some putties are more expensive than others.
- If you choose to do the Social Studies integration about gluep kits, have students calculate a "fair price" for the gluep kits. Remind them to take into account the cost of materials, packaging, and advertising as they determine the price of each kit.
- Have students survey classmates or other students about which type of putty (red, blue, or green) they prefer. Have students tabulate their results and determine the percentage of students who like each type of putty. The results can be posted on a chart or graph.
- Measure the length that a putty can be stretched before it breaks.

Social Studies

- Produce a "putty kit" to sell to other students for holiday presents for siblings. (Be sure that students include safety and disposal information in the kits.) Discuss marketing and pricing issues.

Just for Fun

- Hold a "Putty Olympics" and have students create events for their putties to compete in, such as length of time to flow through a funnel, length it can be stretched, and the highest bounce. Different recipes may "compete" better in different events.

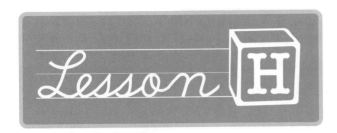

Hide and Seek

Enrich the "Hovering Paper Clip" activity in the book Science Night Family Fun from A to Z *or use as a stand-alone lesson on magnetism.*

Students use the properties of magnetism to move a paper clip through a maze.

Key Science Topic

- magnetism

Average Time Required

Setup	10	minutes
Performance	15–20	minutes
Cleanup	5	minutes

 Overview

National Science Education Standards

Science as Inquiry Standards

- Abilities Necessary to Do Scientific Inquiry
  Students conduct simple investigations to determine what types of materials are attracted to magnets and what materials will interrupt a magnetic field.

  Students discuss what they have learned about magnets with their adult partners and with their classmates.

Physical Science

- Properties of Objects and Materials
  Objects have many observable properties, including attraction to or lack of attraction to a magnet.

  Objects are made of one or more materials and can be described by the properties of the materials from which they are made. Objects containing iron are attracted to magnets.

- Light, Heat, Electricity, and Magnetism
  Magnets attract and repel each other and certain other kinds of materials.

Science and Technology

- Abilities of Technological Design
  Students create paper clip traps according to directions provided. Then they design and test their own traps.

History and Nature of Science

- History of Science
  As early as the sixth century B.C., people observed that magnets are attracted only to certain objects.

94   Classroom Science from 🅐 to 🆉

Science Activity

Materials

paper plates • markers, crayons, pens, or pencils • magnets
• paper clip • tape • scissors • paper

Challenge

Maneuver a paper clip along a crooked path and free it from its trap.

Figure 1

Procedure

Part 1

❶ Draw a crooked path on a paper plate. (See Figure 1.)

❷ Try using the magnet to move the paper clip along the path. (See Figure 2.) Does it make a difference whether the magnet is above or below the paper plate? Try it and find out.

? *What did you observe?*

_____

_____

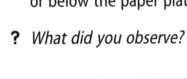

Figure 2

❸ Stack 10 paper plates together. Put your path on top and your magnet on the bottom of the stack. Can you get the paper clip to move now?

? *What did you observe?*

_____

❹ Predict how many paper plates you can stack together and still be able to move the paper clip. Try it and see.

Prediction: _____

Observation: _____

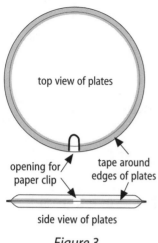

top view of plates

opening for paper clip

tape around edges of plates

side view of plates

Figure 3

Part 2

① Make a paper clip trap by taping two paper plates together as shown in Figure 3. Leave about a 1-inch gap in the tape so you can easily slide a paper clip in and out of this trap. You may want to use a pair of scissors to make this opening a little bigger, but don't make it so big that the paper clip can simply fall out of the trap. Use a marker to draw the location of the "exit."

② Place the paper clip inside the trap.

③ Use your magnet to find the paper clip and free it from the trap.

④ As a team, design your own paper clip trap from another type of container. Figure 4 shows some ideas to get you started. Try your trap to make sure it works. Then challenge other students in the class to free the paper clip from your trap.

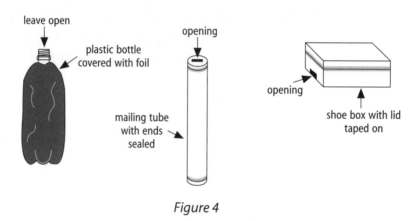

leave open

plastic bottle covered with foil

opening

mailing tube with ends sealed

opening

shoe box with lid taped on

Figure 4

? *Draw a picture of your design and describe how well it worked.*

Teacher Notes for the Science Activity

Materials

- paper plates
- markers, crayons, pens, or pencils
- magnets
- paper clip
- tape
- scissors
- paper

Answers and Observations

❷ *What did you observe?*

The paper clip moves along the path whether the magnet is above the plate or below it.

❸ *What did you observe?*

Unless the magnets are very weak, they will probably move the paper clip even through stacks as thick as ½ inch.

❹ *Observation:*

The strength of the magnets used will control the number of paper plates that can be stacked together and still allow the paper clip to move. This number is typically greater than one, and for strong magnets, the number is high.

Suggestions for Follow-Up

Have your students make a paper clip car tent and see if they can get it to move. Instruct them to do this as follows:

❶ Fold a sheet of paper in thirds and open it back up.

❷ Draw a car on the middle one-third of the paper.

❸ Fold the paper into a tent with the car facing outward, and tape the paper into a triangle.

❹ Attach a paper clip as shown in the diagram.

paper clip

Have students try moving the car along a table using a magnet. They should try holding the magnet above and underneath the table. Have them try using two magnets stuck together and see what happens.

Assessment

Materials

Per student
- magnet
- paper clips
- magnetic marbles

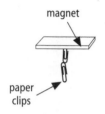

Figure 1

Challenge

Give students the supplies listed above and challenge them, without telling them how, to suspend paper clips in a chain without hooking any of them together. (See Figure 1.) Ask the students to record how many paper clips they can suspend in a row.

Challenge students to suspend as many magnetic marbles in a chain as possible. (See Figure 2.) Have the students record this number. Ask them whether they needed to use the magnet to do this, and discuss the reason why they didn't. (The magnetic marbles have little bar magnets inside them. You might want to take one apart to show this.) Have students write one important fact or idea they learned in this lesson in their science journals.

Figure 2

Science Explanation

This section explains the science concepts in this lesson as well as in the "Hovering Paper Clip" Family Science Challenge in Science Night Family Fun from A to Z. *It is intended for the teacher's information and may be modified as necessary for discussion with students.*

A magnet will attract only certain materials. Most household or classroom objects that are attracted to magnets are made of some alloy containing iron, such as steel. Other materials besides iron also behave this way, but they are less commonly found. Cobalt and nickel are two other metals that can be attracted to magnets. However, don't reach into your pocket to test that five-cent coin, because U.S. "nickels" do not have enough nickel in them to show any magnetic attraction. Being attracted to magnets is not a general property of metals. You can easily check to see that two common metals, aluminum and copper, are not attracted to magnets.

Magnets exert their magnetic force over a certain area, called a magnetic field. The magnetic field extends beyond the magnet itself, and in the Family Science Challenge families learned that this field caused the paper clip to hover. When a thin object that was not attracted to the magnet was passed through the space between the magnet and the paper clip, the magnetic field was uninterrupted and the paper clip continued hovering. When a substance that was attracted to a magnet was passed through the same space, however, the magnetic field was interrupted and the paper clip fell.

In the classroom Science Activity, students discover that it is possible to use the magnet to move the paper clip along the path (even with several paper plates stacked together), because the paper plates are thin and are not attracted to the magnet. The paper plate does not interrupt the magnetic field, so the attraction between the paper clip and magnet is the same as if the paper plate were not between them. Often, a magnet can exert its field through wooden tables, depending on the strength of the magnet and the thickness of the wood.

Any material that is attracted to a magnet can become a magnet itself, either permanently or temporarily, as shown in the Assessment. Materials are attracted to magnets because the materials themselves temporarily become magnetic—or at least some part of them does. Materials not attracted to magnets will not become magnetic.

Cross-Curricular Integration

Art and Music

- Have students make a magnet painting as follows: Place a piece of paper with tempera paint in a box lid. Set a paper clip or magnetic marble on the paint. Drag a magnet on the underside of the box lid to make the paper clip or magnetic marble move through the paint.

Language Arts

- Use magnets to act out a story. Have students cut out story characters from stiff paper and tape small magnets to the back. Create a backdrop for the story, and move the characters around the backdrop using a magnet behind the backdrop.
- Write an acrostic poem for magnets, with each letter representing something a magnet can pick up.
- Read aloud or have students read the following book:
  - *Marta's Magnets*, by Wendy Pfeffer (Silver, ISBN 0382249313)
    Marta's sister Rosa calls her magnet collection junk, but Marta's magnets help her make friends in her new home and help her retrieve a lost key for Rosa's new friend.

Mathematics

- Measure how close a magnet must be to a paper clip to cause the paper clip to move toward it (the place where the magnetic attraction is great enough to overcome friction). Place a paper clip at one edge of a piece of graph paper. Slide a magnet across the paper until the paper clip begins to move toward the magnet. Mark the square where the paper clip first started to move and color in that line back to the magnet. Repeat this several times to get a more precise estimation of where the object first started to move. Test different magnets using the same paper clip.

Social Studies

- Research the importance of magnets to navigation, the historic development of the compass, and how this invention changed exploration.
- Go "orienteering" in the school parking lot or playground. Have students tell how to get from the school to a slide or a specified parking place by using compass directions.

Just for Fun

Use caution when working with iron filings, as they can easily get into students' eyes.

- Create a magnetic toy using a flat yogurt lid, a domed yogurt lid (from a yogurt cup with mix-it-yourself topping), iron filings, and a magnet. Draw a picture or other design on the flat yogurt lid with permanent markers. Place a small amount of iron filings (about $1/16$ teaspoon) on the lid. Snap the domed yogurt lid over the flat lid. Use the magnet to position the iron filings on the design on the flat lid. Alternatively, you can use a Petri dish and lid or a clean Styrofoam® meat tray and plastic wrap to make the toy.

Identity Crisis

*Enrich the **"Inky Elevators"** activity in the book* Science Night Family Fun from A to Z *or use as a stand-alone lesson on chromatography.*

Students try chromatography on different types of paper and on chalk.

. . . . **Key Science Topics**

- capillary action
- chromatography

. . . . **Time Required**

Setup	5	minutes
Performance	15	minutes
Cleanup	5	minutes

·············· National Science Education Standards

Science as Inquiry Standards

- Abilities Necessary to Do Scientific Inquiry

  Students design and conduct an experiment to determine which marker was used to write a message.

  Students conduct investigations using chromatography.

  Students use their observations to develop an explanation for the behavior of the water, paper towels, filter paper, chalk, and inks of different markers.

  Students develop cause-and-effect relationships about chromatographs and the different markers and media used to create them.

  Students share their observations and investigations with their adult partners and with their classmates.

Physical Science

- Properties of Objects and Materials

  Water-based ink is a mixture of water and one or more dyes. The properties of the components of this solution can be used to separate the dyes.

  Objects have the property of being porous, which has to do with the size and quantity of the object's holes, or "pores."

  Porous objects like chalk and paper allow water and other liquids to flow through them easily.

- Position and Motion of Objects

  In chromatography, the positions of the separated materials are described relative to the position of the solvent.

History and Nature of Science

- Science as a Human Endeavor

  Scientists developed and use the process of chromatography to help identify substances.

Science Activity

Materials

strips of white paper towels • several different colors of water-soluble markers • water • plastic cup • sharpened pencil • crayons • strips of filter paper • piece of porous (cheap, not dustless) white chalk

Challenge

Can you discover how the ink moves?

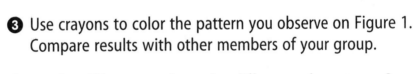

Procedure

❶ Pour about ¼ inch of water into the cup. Each person in the group should select a different color of marker and then use that marker for all parts of this activity. Record the color of the marker you are using on the dotted line in Figure 1.

❷ Do the paper towel chromatography with your marker as you learned in the Family Science Challenge. Use a pencil to write the color of your marker above the pencil hole on your paper strip. If you didn't do the Family Science Challenge, follow your teacher's instructions.

❸ Use crayons to color the pattern you observe on Figure 1. Compare results with other members of your group.

? *Do the different markers give different color patterns?*

_____

_____

_____

❹ Repeat step 2 with a filter-paper strip and the same marker. Draw the pattern you observe on Figure 2.

? *Do the different papers make a difference in the patterns?*

_____

_____

Figure 1

Figure 2

❺ Use your marker to draw a ring about ½ inch from one end of a fresh stick of chalk as shown in Figure 3. Also color in the line on Figure 3 with your marker.

? *What do you think will happen if you stand the chalk, ring end down, in the water?*

_____

_____

_____

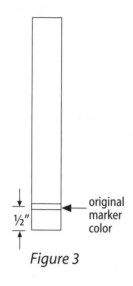

← original marker color

½"

Figure 3

❻ Stand your piece of chalk, ring end down, in the water. (See Figure 4.) The marker ring must be above the water level. Observe the chalk for a few minutes.

? *What happens?*

_____

_____

_____

marker ring

← water

Figure 4

❼ When the water has almost reached the top of the chalk, remove the chalk from the cup of water. Color in the picture of the chalk (Figure 5) with crayons so it looks like your piece of chalk after you removed it from the water.

❽ Let the chalk dry overnight. Try using it to draw a picture on a sheet of white paper.

? *What do you see?*

_____

_____

_____

Figure 5

Teacher Notes for the Science Activity

Materials

Per group
- paper towels
- several colors of water-soluble markers
- water
- clear 12-ounce plastic cup
- sharpened pencil
- crayons
- coffee filter or filter paper
- porous white chalk

Resources

Water-soluble pens made for overhead projectors, such as the Vis-a-Vis® brand, or watercolor markers, such as the Mr. Sketch® markers, work well with this activity. Some brands of washable markers do not work as well. Black, brown, or purple markers usually provide the best range of colors during the chromatography. Red, blue, and yellow markers usually will not separate at all and should not be used.

Setup

Cut the paper towels and the coffee filters or filter paper into 1-inch-wide strips. The strips should be approximately 1 inch longer than the height of the cups the students will be using.

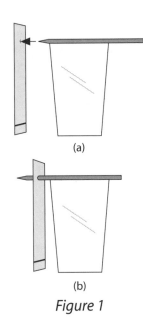

(a)

(b)

Figure 1

Procedure for Paper Towel Chromatography

❶ Use a pencil to draw a horizontal line about ½ inch above the bottom edge of one paper towel strip. Use a water-soluble marker to trace along the pencil line.

❷ Hold the strip next to the clear plastic cup so that the bottom edge of the strip almost reaches the bottom of the cup. Push the point of a pencil through the top of the strip exactly even with the rim of the cup. (See Figures 1a and 1b.)

❸ Lift the pencil from the cup and push the paper to the middle of the pencil. Continue to hold the pencil while your partner pours about ¼ inch of water into the cup.

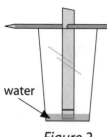

water

Figure 2

❹ Set the pencil across the rim of the cup so that the bottom of the paper is in the water. The marker line should be above the water. (See Figure 2.) If the marker line accidentally dips below the water level, discard the paper, rinse out the cup, and start over.

❺ Observe the water and the marker line.

❻ When the water gets up near the top of the cup, remove the strip from the water and lay it on a paper towel to dry.

Answers and Observations

❸ *Do the different markers give different color patterns?*

Yes, the different brands and different colors produce different separations.

❹ *Do the different papers make a difference in the patterns?*

Yes, the paper-towel pattern is typically more blurry than the pattern on filter paper.

❻ *What happens?*

The marker ink should separate into its component colors as the water moves up the chalk.

❽ *What do you see?*

The color from the chalk is transferred to the paper.

Suggestions for Follow-Up

Have students discuss where they think the colors they observed came from. The class can compare the patterns they observed on the paper towel, filter paper, and chalk.

Assessment

Materials

Per class
- many different brands of black water-soluble markers
- scissors

Per student
- test strip of filter paper
- extra strips of coffee filter or filter paper
- 8-ounce clear plastic cup
- sharpened pencil
- water

Setup

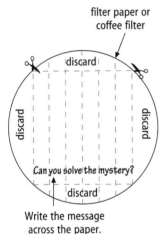

filter paper or coffee filter

Write the message across the paper.

- Prepare test strips for students as follows. Choose one of the black water-soluble markers to write a message in short, wide letters (to simulate a line) across the coffee filter or filter paper ½ inch from the bottom, and remember which brand of marker you used. (See figure.)

- Cut the marked filter paper into 1-inch-wide strips. The strips should be about 1 inch longer than the height of the cup you are using. Discard any that are not long enough. Prepare enough strips for each student to have one with part of the test message written on it and distribute them to the class.

- Cut enough extra strips of filter paper for each student the have four or five blank strips. Distribute them to the class.

Challenge

Challenge students to design an experiment to discover which marker was used to write the message on the test strip of filter paper. By doing their own separations with the different brands of marker and comparing these to the separation pattern of the message on the test strips, can students tell which marker was used to write the message? Have them explain why they chose the marker they did, using the results of the chromatography test to support their reasoning. Have students describe their experiments and write one important fact or idea they learned about chromatography in their science journals.

Science Explanation

This section explains the science concepts in this lesson as well as in the "Inky Elevators" Family Science Challenge in Science Night Family Fun from A to Z. *It is intended for the teacher's information and may be modified for discussion with students.*

Water-soluble ink appears to be a single color. However, the ink usually contains mixtures of different-colored pigments. In the Family Science Challenge, families learned that these pigments can be separated by a technique called "chromatography." The separation medium requires a stationary phase (the paper or chalk) and a mobile phase (the water).

In the classroom Science Activity, students perform paper and chalk chromatography. The solvent (water) and the ink of the marker move through the stationary phase because of capillary action. Paper and chalk are porous, which means they are full of tiny holes, or capillaries. These capillaries make the materials absorbent. Capillary action allows the water or other solvent to move up the paper or chalk above the level of liquid in the cup. If you have ever had a blood test, the blood from a finger prick was probably drawn into a very narrow glass tube (called a capillary tube). This is another example of capillary action.

The water-soluble components of the inks placed on the paper or chalk dissolve in water. As the water moves up the strip, the water-soluble ink pigments are carried along. The separation that results depends on the differences in solubility and other characteristics of the pigments. In general, the pigments that are more soluble in water are more strongly attracted to water and move up the paper or chalk at a faster rate than those that are less soluble and have a smaller degree of attraction for the water. Different brands of ink contain different combinations of pigments, which result in different separation patterns, as students saw in the Assessment. The number and size of the capillaries in the stationary phase also affects the separation. Because different papers have different compositions, they often give separations of different quality. For example, chromatography filter paper or other filter paper allows slower but more vivid results than paper towels or coffee filters.

Crime laboratories use chromatography to separate the components of substances for clues leading to the identification of these substances. For example, they might use chromatography to identify the ink used to write a ransom note.

Cross-Curricular Integration

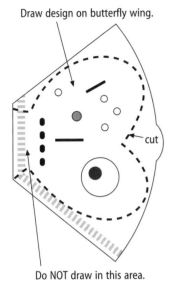

Draw design on butterfly wing.

cut

Do NOT draw in this area.

Art and Music

- Have students make chromatography butterflies as follows: Cut a cone-style coffee filter into the shape of a butterfly. Draw half of a butterfly on one side of the filter, with the "body" being the small, flat edge. Have students use water-soluble markers to draw a design on the butterfly wing. Students should copy this design into their Science Journals to use as a reference. Place the butterfly, body end down, in a cup with a small amount of water. The water should come to just below the design on the butterfly when it is in the cup. Observe the color pattern and remove the butterfly before the water reaches the edge. Set the butterfly on a paper towel to dry.
- Use chromatography to decorate fabric pieces in patterns. Thin cotton blends work well. Students can use these pieces for bookmarks or sew and stuff them to make small pincushions or tooth pillows.
- Talk about primary and secondary colors and how white, gray, and black can affect them. A good resource is *Color Dance,* by Ann Jonas (Greenwillow, ISBN 0688-05991-0).

Language Arts

- Have students write a simple mystery that is solved by chromatography.
- Have students write a story about a world that was once filled with only the color black. Describe what this world was like and how the world was able to change into one filled with all the colors of today.
- Write a story about a world that once had no black. How was the color discovered? How did the world change after the discovery of black?
- Read aloud or have students read one or more of the following books:
  - *The Black Snowman,* by Phil Mendez (Scholastic, ISBN 0590448730)
    Jacob and his brother make a snowman from the dirty city snow. The boys wrap the snowman in a colorful cloth they find. But the scrap is really a kente, an African storyteller's shawl, which has magical qualities the boys soon discover.
  - *Color,* by Ruth Heller (Scholastic, ISBN 0-590-69172)
    This books talks about colors and how they are combined in the printing process. It is an excellent resource because it uses the true colors of magenta, cyan blue, and yellow. It is very effective visually because it uses overlays to show mixing of colors.
  - *From the Mixed-Up Files of Mrs. Basil E. Frankweiler,* by E.L. Konigsburg (Yearling, ISBN 0-440-4318-08)
    This story incorporates detective techniques including chromatography.
  - *Hailstones and Halibut Bones,* by Mary O'Neil (Doubleday, ISBN 0385-41078-6)
    A classic book of poetry about colors.

Life Science

- Use celery in colored water to show how water moves up plant stems to the leaves. Pick a piece of celery with leaves, cut off a stalk with a sharp knife, and immediately place it in undiluted liquid food color (red works well). Have students predict and then observe how the color moves by observing the changes in the celery. The amount of time this process takes depends on the length of the celery stick—allow about ½ hour for a 6-inch piece. You can break the celery stalk open to allow the food coloring inside the xylem and the phloem to be more visible. Try doing the activity with a white carnation; be sure to cut the stem immediately before you place it in the food color.
- Investigate more about dyes and their importance through history. How were dyes obtained? What colors were considered valuable and why? How successful was color mixing in dye making?

Mathematics

- Use a stopwatch or a clock with a second hand to measure the time it takes the water to move a set distance (for example, 1½ inches) up different types of paper. Graph the results.

Social Studies

- Invite a crime-lab scientist to talk to the class about how chromatography is used in studying clues.
- Investigate more about dyes and their importance through history. How were dyes obtained? What colors were considered valuable and why? How successful was color mixing in dye making?

Lesson J

Just Call Me

*Enrich the **"Jive Jabberwackies"** activity in the book* Science Night Family Fun from A to Z *or use as a stand-alone lesson on frequency and sound waves.*

Students investigate how different strings carry sound vibrations.

Key Science Topics

- frequency
- hearing
- sound
- waves
- wavelength

Average Time Required

Setup	15	minutes
Performance	15–20	minutes
Cleanup	5	minutes

 Overview

. . . . **National Science Education Standards**

Science as Inquiry Standards

- Abilities Necessary to Do Scientific Inquiry
  Students conduct a simple investigation to test how the size of the Jabberwacky affects its pitch.

  Students listen to different-sized Jabberwackies and use their observations to construct a reasonable explanation of the relationship between the size of the amplifier (cup) and the pitch of the Jabberwacky.

  Students predict the sounds different types of string will make when used in their Jabberwackies.

  Students test their predictions by making systematic observations using different types of string in their Jabberwackies.

  Students discuss and demonstrate the different Jabberwackies with their adult partners, teacher, and classmates.

Physical Science

- Position and Motion of Objects
  Sound in the Jabberwacky is produced by a vibrating string.

- Transfer of Energy
  Mechanical energy can be transferred into sound energy.

History and Nature of Science

- History of Science
  Students research the history of telephones and long-distance communication.

  Students learn about the history of various musical instruments.

Science Activity

Materials

2 disposable paper cups • plastic yarn needle • 18-inch lengths of various types of string • 4 paper clips • 2 squares of fabric • water

Challenge

Can you discover how different types of string change the sound of the Jabberwacky?

Procedure

paper clip

pull

Figure 1

Work in pairs for this activity.

❶ Use the plastic yarn needle to poke a small hole in the bottom of each of the two cups. Be careful not to poke yourself.

❷ Make a Jabberwacky for each partner by feeding one end of an 18-inch length of cotton string through the bottom of a cup. Anchor the string in the cup by tying a paper clip to the end of the string and pulling it tight back into the cup. (See Figure 1.)

❸ Use both dry and moistened fabric squares and what you learned in the Family Science Challenge to make the Jabberwackies squawk. If you didn't do the Family Science Challenge, follow the instructions given by your teacher.

? *Does the sound have a high or low pitch? Record your observations in the Observation Table on the next page.*

❹ Use the same cup you used above, but try different string materials to determine whether they can be used to produce different pitches of sound. Also, compare the sound each string makes when the fabric square is dry and when it is wet.

? *Record your observations in the Observation Table. How do the pitches compare to the pitch with the cotton string?*

Observation Table		
Type of String	Dry Fabric (High or low pitch?)	Wet Fabric (High or low pitch?)
cotton string		

5 With your partner, decide which string gave the best sound. Take a piece of that type of string and put it through your cup. Attach a paper clip to both ends of the string. Your partner should do the same. (See Figure 2.)

6 Make a "phone" by linking the two free-hanging paper clips together and standing with your cups to your ears so that the string is pulled tight between you and your partner. (See Figure 3.) Pluck the string.

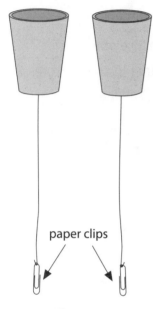

paper clips

Figure 2

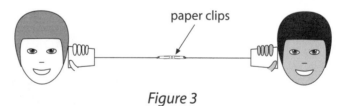

paper clips

Figure 3

? *What do you observe when you pluck the string?*

_____

_____

_____

7 Keep your cup to your ear while your partner talks into the other cup. Take turns talking and listening.

? *What do you observe?*

_____

_____

_____

Teacher Notes for the Science Activity

Materials

Per class
• water

Per pair of students
• plastic yarn needle
• 2 disposable 12-ounce or smaller paper cups
• various types of string (2 pieces of each—see Resources)
• 4 paper clips
• pieces of fabric such as denim

Resources

Use pieces of yarn, twine, thread, fishing line, cord, shoelaces, wire, or any other "strings" you can think of. You'll need 18-inch lengths of the different types of string. The fabric squares can be cut from old blue jeans, or you can reuse the pieces from the Family Science Challenge.

Plastic yarn needles are available in fabric or craft stores.

Setup

• For primary students, punch the holes in the cups in advance.
• You may wish to tie the strings to the paper clips in advance.
• Cut the string samples into pieces about 18 inches long. Cut two pieces of each type of string for each pair of students.
• Cut the fabric into pieces about 2 inches by 2 inches. (The exact dimensions are not critical.)

Answers and Observations

❻ *What do you observe when you pluck the string?*
A sound is produced.

❼ *What do you observe?*
The sound of the speaker's voice travels through the string and out the cup.

Suggestions for Follow-Up

As a class, compare results. Which strings produced the highest pitch? Which produced the lowest pitch?

Assessment

Materials

Per student
- Jabberwacky toy used in the Science Activity
- string that produced the best sound in the Science Activity
- water
- different types of fabric

Challenge

Challenge students to determine the effects that different fabrics have on their Jabberwacky toys. Have students use the type of string that produced the best sound in the Science Activity. Instruct students to use different fabrics to pull along the string. Try them wet and dry.

Have students construct an Observation Table like the one below in their science journals. What effect does the fabric have on the sound? Which fabrics did the class decide gave the best results? Were wet fabrics more effective than dry ones? End by having students write one important fact or idea they learned during this lesson in their science journals.

Observation Table		
Type of Fabric	Dry Fabric (High or low pitch?)	Wet Fabric (High or low pitch?)

Science Explanation

This section explains the science concepts in this lesson as well as in the "Jive Jabberwackies" Family Science Challenge in Science Night Family Fun from A to Z. *It is intended for the teacher's information and may be modified as necessary for discussion with students.*

Hearing is the process of picking up and interpreting wavelike air-pressure disturbances we call sound waves. These waves are produced when a physical force (such as the plucking of a string, the beating of a drum, or air traveling over human vocal cords) causes an object to vibrate, which in turn causes the surrounding air particles to vibrate. These vibrations produce sound waves, which are funneled into the ear.

As families discovered in the Family Science Challenge, pulling on a string sets up many vibrations in the string but causes very little air to move. When the string is attached to the cup, the vibrations are transmitted to the cup. Due to both its size and shape, the vibrating cup is able to move much more air and produce a louder sound.

A damp cloth works better than a dry one because it produces more friction with the string. The friction causes the cloth to move with small start-stop-start-stop motions rather than sliding freely. This produces more vibration in the string, thus causing the "clucking" sound.

The pitch of sounds depends on the frequency of the vibrating sound waves—the higher the frequency, the higher the pitch. Frequency is a precise scientific term meaning the number of wave cycles that pass a receiving point each second. The frequency of a vibrating sound wave depends on the wavelength of the vibrations—the shorter the wavelength, the higher the frequency. (See figure at left.) Frequency is measured in cycles per second, or hertz. The human ear most easily detects frequencies between 1,000 and 4,000 hertz. The range of hearing in young children extends from approximately 20 hertz to 20,000 hertz, and usually the range decreases with age.

Pitch is a more complicated term related to frequency, but it also depends on the way our ears and brains perceive sound. The smaller cups and strings produce shorter wavelengths, higher frequencies, and higher pitches than the larger cups.

Vibrations having many different wavelengths are produced by pulling on a string. Not all of these wavelengths are affected by the cup. The cup has a natural tendency to vibrate with certain wavelengths determined by the size, shape, and material of which the cup is made. These wavelengths are easily transmitted from the string to the cup. For larger cups, the wavelength of the natural vibrations is longer and the frequency is lower. Thus, the larger the cup, the lower the pitch.

Different types of string vibrate differently. This means different wavelengths and frequencies, and thus different sounds, will be produced.

wavelength

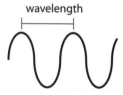

shorter wavelength,
greater frequency,
higher pitch

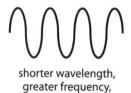

longer wavelength,
lower frequency,
lower pitch

Cross-Curricular Integration

Art and Music

- Have the music teacher bring in a variety of stringed instruments to demonstrate to the class. Identify the amplifier in each case. How is the pitch related to the size of the instrument?
- Create rubber band instruments with assorted sizes of rubber bands stretched over pencil boxes or other containers. Try to keep the containers the same size so that students can focus on the size of the rubber bands, the factor that is responsible for the differences in sound.

Home, Safety, and Career

- Discuss the discomfort and dangers caused by loud noises, including loud music.

Language Arts

- Read aloud or have students read one or more of the following books:
  - *Sound, Heat, and Light: Energy at Work*, by Melvin Berger (Scholastic, ISBN 0590461036)
    This book is an interesting example of nonfiction for students to use to find out more information on a topic of study. The sound chapter provides information and activities to illustrate concepts of sound.
  - *I have a Sister, My Sister is Deaf*, by Jean Whitehouse (Harper Trophy, ISBN 0060247010)
    A young girl describes how her deaf sister experiences everyday things. Because a deaf person's ears can't amplify sound, they experience sound through vibrations.
- Discuss and chart "high," "medium," and "low" sounds. (Examples include siren, speaking voice, growl.)

Social Studies

- Study the history of communications over long distances, including technologies such as drums, telegraph, and telephones.
- Research the history of a stringed instrument such as a violin, banjo, harp, or dulcimer. You may want to have students focus on stringed instruments from different countries and cultures.

Just for Fun

- Play a class song using Jabberwackies with different-sized cups and different types of string.

Knots and Swirls

Enrich the **"Kooky Pencils"** *activity in the book* Science Night Family Fun from A to Z *or use as a stand-alone lesson on hydrophobic substances and surface tension.*

Students use a traditional Japanese art form to create swirled ink patterns on paper.

. . . . **Key Science Topics**

- mixtures
- surface tension
- hydrophobic and hydrophilic

. . . . **Average Time Required**

Science Activity

Setup	10	minutes
Performance	20	minutes
Cleanup	10	minutes

Overview

National Science Education Standards

Science as Inquiry Standards

- Abilities Necessary to Do Scientific Inquiry

  Students conduct simple investigations that relate to the properties of water and hydrophobic substances as well as the concept of density.

  Students develop explanations about why the ink and paint adhere to the pencils and paper.

  Students develop cause-and-effect relationships about the intensity of the ink on the paper and the ink-and-oil pattern in the water.

  Students analyze their explanations and those of their classmates during class discussions.

  Students share their observations and explanations with their adult partners and with their classmates.

Physical Science

- Properties of Objects and Materials

  Hydrophobic substances, like oil and carbon, do not easily mix with water.

  Oil is less dense than water and floats on top of water.

  The carbon used in india ink, like the carbon used in graphite pencils, is attracted to paper.

  The surface tension of water is high. This surface tension allows the fine particles of carbon in the india ink to float on the water.

- Position and Motion of Objects

  The concentric circles of carbon and oil can be pushed by adding a drop of either oil or carbon or by gently swirling them.

History and Nature of Science

- Science as a Human Endeavor

  The art and science of suminagashi has been practiced in Japan for many centuries.

Science Activity

Materials

newspaper • Styrofoam® or plastic plate or bowl • water • cotton swab halves • permanent-type india ink • stirring stick or toothpick • art-quality drawing paper • basin or sink • (optional) paint smocks or aprons

Challenge

Can you use oil and water to create a swirling ink pattern on paper?

Procedure

Be very careful to avoid getting the ink on your clothes or hands because it will stain.

❶ Prepare the work surface by covering it with newspaper. If paint smocks or aprons are available, put one on over your clothes.

❷ Place the plate or bowl on the newspaper and half-fill it with water.

❸ BARELY dip the tip of a clean cotton swab into the ink. You need only a VERY small amount of ink for the investigation.

❹ Use a QUICK "touch-and-remove" action to BARELY touch the inky swab to the center of the water's surface. IMMEDIATELY withdraw the swab.

? *What do you observe?*

_____

_____

❺ Rub the tip of the second clean cotton swab across your forehead or nose to smudge a bit of skin oil onto the swab.

❻ Use a QUICK "touch-and-remove" action to touch the oily swab to the center of the spreading ink.

? *What do you observe?*

_____

_____

7 Without putting more ink and oil on your swabs, use the QUICK "touch-and-remove" action to continue this application of first the ink, then the oil, to the center of the water several times.

? *What do you observe?*

_____

_____

8 Use a stirring stick or toothpick to VERY GENTLY swirl the surface of the water to make a pattern with the ink.

9 Use a pencil to write your name on the back of a piece of art paper. Pencil lead is made of carbon, the same material in the india ink.

Figure 1

10 Gently lay the piece of art-quality drawing paper on the water. (See Figure 1.) If the corners curl up, gently tap them down so they touch the surface of the water. Lift the paper off the surface. Let the paper drip for a moment, then lay the resulting artwork flat (ink side up) in the designated place to dry.

? *What do you observe?*

_____

_____

_____

11 Throw the used swabs in the trash and empty the plate or bowl of oil, ink, and water into the basin or sink.

Teacher Notes
for the Science Activity

Materials

For setup only
* scissors

Per class
* large basin or sink
* trash can

Per group
* Styrofoam® or plastic plate or bowl
* newspapers
* water
* cotton-tipped swabs
* permanent-type india ink
* stirring sticks or toothpicks
* art-quality drawing paper
* (optional) paint smocks or aprons

Setup

* Cut the cotton-tipped swabs in half with scissors.

* Cut the sheets of drawing paper into four equal pieces approximately 4¼ x 5½ inches. Cut enough sheets to allow students to make a second suminagashi design if possible.

* To prevent disappointment, test the activity in advance with your drawing paper, ink, and Styrofoam or plastic plate or bowl to make sure that the ink doesn't sink and that it transfers with a minimum of smearing. If the ink sinks, try another brand. If too much smearing occurs, try different paper.

* Decide how you will supply water for the activity. If necessary, fill tubs or bottles with water for students to use, and provide buckets for waste water.

* Spread newspapers on and around the work area, and have students wear old clothing or aprons. The india ink can stain clothing and furniture. Extra care should be taken to prevent the ink from staining.

Answers and Observations

❹ *What do you observe?*

The ink spreads over the surface of the water in a circular pattern.

❻ *What do you observe?*

The oil spreads out and pushes the ink farther out.

❼ *What do you observe?*

The ink and oil form concentric rings.

❿ *What do you observe?*

The pattern made by the ink and oil is transferred to the paper.

Suggestions for Follow-Up

Have all groups compare their patterns with the patterns created by other groups. Are all the black areas equally dark? If not, what might have caused the differences? Discuss the significance of the statement in step 9 that pencil lead is made of carbon, just as the india ink is. (Both adhere to paper.)

References

Chambers, A. *Suminagashi;* Thames and Hudson: London, 1991; pp 6–16.

Sarquis, J.L.; Sarquis, M.; Williams, J.P. "Sumi Nagashi"; *Teaching Chemistry with TOYS: Activities for Grades K–9;* McGraw-Hill: New York, 1995; pp 189–194.

Sarquis, M.; Woodward, L. "Suminagashi Greeting Cards for Grandparent's Day," *Science Projects for Holidays Throughout the Year;* McGraw-Hill: New York, 1998; pp 33–44.

Shakhashiri, B.Z. *Chemical Demonstrations, A Handbook for Teachers of Chemistry,* University of Wisconsin, Madison, WI: 1989, Vol. 3; pp 301–304, 358–359.

Suzuki, C. Dept of Education, Shiga University, Hiratsu, Ohtsu, Shiga Japan. Abstract P3.35, 11th International Conference on Chemical Education: York, England, August 1991.

Assessment

Materials

Per group or student
- a few small pieces of white paper
- cup
- Styrofoam® or plastic plate or bowl
- water
- cinnamon
- ground black pepper
- dish detergent
- cotton-tipped swab

Challenge

Through a class discussion, bring out the idea that the india ink used to make the marbled designs is actually a very fine powder that rests on the surface of the water because of surface tension. Challenge students to apply what they learned about making marbled prints with india ink to the task of making prints with powdered cinnamon or pepper. Show them the materials they have available, and ask them to come up with a plan. Have students try out their ideas and record the results. Give them a chance to try a new approach if they are not satisfied with the results. When all of the students have tested their ideas, have them share their methods and results. After discussing the results as a class, have students write one fact or idea they learned during this lesson in their science journals.

Science Explanation

This section explains the science concepts in this lesson as well as in the "Kooky Pencils" Family Activity in Science Night Family Fun from A to Z. *It is intended for the teacher's information and may be modified as necessary for discussion with students.*

In the Family Science Challenge, oil-based model paint is dropped into water, where it floats because of two important factors: 1) oil does not mix with water (in other words, oil and water are immiscible), and 2) oil is less dense than water (thus the oil floats on top of the water). When the toothpick and pencil are pushed through the film of oil paint, attractive forces cause the paint to adhere to the surfaces of these objects.

In the classroom Science Activity, students use india ink, which is similar to the sumi, or black ink, used in Japanese art. India ink is a special mixture of extremely fine particles of a black pigment suspended in water. The black pigment is either carbon black or lampblack, which are both chiefly forms of carbon. When a small amount of india ink is placed on the surface of the water, the finely divided particles of black pigment spread out, forming a very thin carbon layer on the water's surface. The pigment floats because of two important factors: 1) carbon and water do not mix under normal conditions, and 2) the very fine pieces of carbon float on top of the water because of water's high surface tension. Although carbon black and lampblack are actually more dense than water, the surface tension of water makes them float. The water acts like it has a skin over it, so it can support some materials that are more dense than it is, especially if these materials are fine particles.

The fact that mixing does not occur when either oil and water are combined or the carbon black/lampblack pigment and water are combined is because the attractive forces that exist within water and within oil (or carbon black/lampblack) are greater than the attractive forces that would exist between the oil (or carbon black/lampblack) and water if they were to mix. In fact, both the black pigment and the oil are said to be hydrophobic ("hydro" meaning "water" and "phobic" meaning "fearing"). Hydrophobic substances are not attracted to and do not mix with water. Conversely, a substance that is attracted to water is hydrophilic ("philic" meaning "loving").

In the classroom Science Activity, the presence of both ink and oil prevents either material from completely spreading out. Thus, as drops of ink and oil are placed alternately on the water, they form a series of concentric circles. Gently swirling the water's surface disturbs the symmetrical pattern of the circles but does not allow the separated oil and ink to join up. Thus, a swirled pattern results. The pattern can be transferred to paper because the black pigment is attracted to the paper. When the paper is laid on the water's surface, the carbon adheres to the paper, maintaining its swirled pattern. Another familiar form of carbon, the graphite used in "lead" pencils, has a similar affinity for paper.

The classroom Science Activity is an example of Suminagashi (meaning "spilled ink"), which is a process of floating ink patterns on the surface of water and transferring the patterns to paper. Sumi, or Chinese ink, made from pine soot, is a traditional material but not necessarily the only ink used. Because one property of water is that it is always moving, no two suminagashi designs can ever be exactly alike.

Cross-Curricular Integration

Art

- Further investigate the process of marbling. Many techniques and strategies can be used to print designs on paper. Kits are available from Educational Innovations, 888/912-7474, and many local arts and crafts stores.

Home, Safety, and Career

- Take a class field trip to a printing company, or have a printer visit the class and talk about different printing methods.

Language Arts

- Have students make suminagashi or marbled paper and write a letter on it to someone special.
- Look for books of folktales with illustrations that incorporate Oriental brush painting or suminagashi techniques.

Social Studies

- Research the history of suminagashi and the ways the products were used.

Lucky Penny Drop

*Enrich the **"Lincoln Drops"** activity in the book* Science Night Family Fun from A to Z *or use as a stand-alone lesson on water and surface tension.*

Students investigate surface tension in plain water and soapy water.

. . . .
Key Science Topics

- cohesion
- surface tension
- water and its properties

. . . .
Average Time Required

Setup	5	minutes
Performance	15	minutes
Cleanup	5	minutes

.... ## National Science Education Standards

Science as Inquiry Standards

- Abilities Necessary to Do Scientific Inquiry
  Students predict how many pennies can be added to a "full" cup of plain water and how many pennies can be added to a "full" cup of soapy water.

  Students conduct a simple experiment to determine how many pennies can be added to a "full" cup of water before it spills over.

  Students compare the shapes of the water and soapy water on the penny and the number of drops of each that will fit on the penny. They use their observations to construct a reasonable explanation of the differences.

  Students design an experiment to determine whether adding soap to the water will affect their previous results.

  Students discuss their results with their adult partners and classmates.

Physical Science

- Properties of Objects and Materials
  Water and soapy water have observable characteristic properties. The two liquids behave differently due to differences in their surface tensions.

History and Nature of Science

- History of Science
  Students learn about the history of soap-making and soap use.

Science Activity

Materials

2 small, clear plastic cups • pennies • water • dishwashing liquid • tray • dropper

Challenge

Can you predict and then determine how many pennies can be added to a "full" cup of water?

Procedure

➤ *Do not drink the water in this activity.*

❶ Place a cup on the tray. Fill the cup with water so that the water is level with the top surface of the cup. Draw a picture of what the water level looks like in the cup in Figure 1.

❷ Predict how many pennies you can add to the cup before the water spills over. Record your prediction in the Observation Table below. Try the experiment and record your findings.

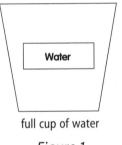

full cup of water

Figure 1

Observation Table		
Plain Water		
Prediction:		
Trial	# of objects	Description of how pennies were added
1		
2		
3		
4		

❸ Determine whether the way you add the pennies affects the results by repeating the experiment several more times. Be sure to start with the cup filled to the same starting level for each trial. Record the number of pennies the cup of water could hold and note the way you added the pennies. Draw a picture of what the water level looked like just before it overflowed in Figure 2.

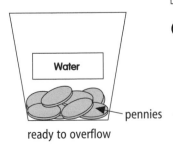

ready to overflow

Figure 2

full cup of soapy water

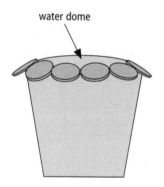

pennies

ready to overflow

Figure 3

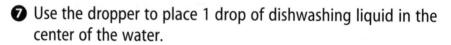

water dome

Figure 4

4 Design an experiment to determine whether adding dishwashing liquid to the water will affect the results you found in steps 2 and 3. Then try it and find out.

? *What did you do? What did you find out?*

_____

_____

_____

5 In Figure 3, draw what the cup of soapy water looked like before the pennies were added and just before it overflowed.

6 Fill a cup with water (not soapy) so that the water level is slightly above the rim of the cup. Balance pennies around the rim of the cup as shown in Figure 4.

7 Use the dropper to place 1 drop of dishwashing liquid in the center of the water.

? *What happens?*

_____

_____

_____

Teacher Notes for the Science Activity

Materials

Per student or group
- 2 small, clear plastic cups
- pennies
- water
- dishwashing liquid
- tray, such as a cafeteria tray, plastic plate, or aluminum pan
- dropper
- (optional) colander

A colander is useful for separating and rinsing the pennies.

Answers and Observations

Draw pictures of the water levels.

full cup of water   ready to overflow

full cup of
soapy water   ready to overflow

❼ What happens?

The pennies fall in.

Suggestions for Follow-Up

Have students compare the water levels they drew in steps 1 and 3. How are they different? How do these tap water levels compare with the soapy water levels from step 5? Which liquid allowed students to place more pennies in it before it spilled? Why might this be?

Assessment

Materials

Per class
- water
- dishwashing liquid
- red and blue food color
- 2 dropper bottles or 2 cups with droppers
- cup and teaspoon measures
- masking tape and marker for labels
- scissors

Per student or group
- 3-inch x 3-inch piece of waxed paper
- a few drops of "Unknown A" (colored water; prepared in Setup)
- a few drops of "Unknown B" (colored soap-water solution; prepared in Setup)

Setup

- Prepare "Unknown A" by adding several drops of red food color to a dropper bottle or cup of water. Label the dropper bottle or cup "Unknown A."

- Prepare "Unknown B" by measuring 1 cup of water into a dropper bottle or cup. Stir 1 teaspoon dishwashing liquid into the water. Allow this solution to settle completely before using it in class so no bubbles remain to give away the identity of the solution. Label the cup or dropper bottle "Unknown B."

- Cut the waxed paper into 3-inch x 3-inch squares.

Challenge

Challenge the students to identify which unknown solution is pure water and which is soapy water by looking at a few drops of each liquid. Give each student a piece of waxed paper and carefully drop a few drops of each liquid onto the paper. Be careful not to shake the bottles and cause bubbles or sudsing in the soap-water solution.

Have students study how the drops behave, record their observations, then choose which drop is the water and which is the soap-water solution. Ask them to record what behaviors of the drops caused them to make these decisions. Have students share their observations and reasons for their decision with the class, then have students write one important fact or idea they learned during this lesson in their science journals.

Science Explanation

This section explains the science concepts in this lesson as well as in the "Lincoln Drops" Family Science Challenge in Science Night Family Fun from A to Z. *It is intended for the teacher's information and may be modified as necessary for discussion with students.*

Both the Family Science Challenge and the classroom Science Activity investigate the surface tension of water and how it is affected by adding soap. Surface tension is the phenomenon that causes water to act like it has a thin, invisible "skin" on its surface and to bead up when dropped onto a waterproof surface, form a dome on the head of a penny, or form a dome over the rim of a cup.

The high surface tension of water results from the very strong attraction water molecules have for each other. This tendency for particles of a liquid to be attracted to each other is called cohesion. The figure below illustrates the cohesive forces in a drop of water. Water molecules in the middle of a drop or cup of water are attracted equally in all directions. These water molecules on the surface, however, are attracted only to the water molecules within the sample. This attraction causes the dome you see on the head of the penny and in the cup. Water molecules are not attracted to the air that surrounds the outer layer. This figure is an extremely simplified representation; a drop of water actually contains an almost unimaginable number (something like 2,000,000,000,000,000,000,000) of water molecules, which are continually slipping and sliding over and around one another.

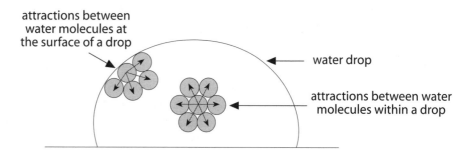

The surface tension of water can be reduced by adding soap or dishwashing liquid. Soap is a type of surfactant (a surface-acting agent), a substance that interferes with the attractive forces between the water molecules. Soapy water does not form a dome like pure water does. Rather, it spreads out over more of the surface. In the Family Science Challenge, families found that they couldn't add as many drops of soapy water to the penny as they could with just tap water. In the Science Activity, students found that fewer pennies could be put into the cup of soapy water before it overflowed.

In the Assessment, students are asked to distinguish between the soapy water drops and the tap water drops. They can do this by observing the drops on waxed paper and comparing their observations to the pictures they drew in the Science Activity. As they observed in the Science Activity, the drops of soapy water will not form domes like the tap water drops do.

Cross-Curricular Integration

Earth Science

• Observe the shapes of dewdrops on leaves or on newly waxed cars.

Language Arts

• Read aloud or have students read the following book:
  ○ *A Drop of Water,* by Walter Wick (Scholastic, ISBN 0590221973)
    Photographer Wick, best known as the illustrator of the I Spy *picture book series, uses simple techniques to show water properties such as surface tension, adhesion, capillary attraction, molecular motion, freezing, evaporation, and condensation.*

Life Science

• Have students study water striders and how they move across the surface of water.

Social Studies

• Soap works well as a cleaning agent in part because it breaks the surface tension of water. Research the history of soapmaking and soap use.

Just for Fun

• Do one or more of the following demonstrations for the class:
  ○ Sprinkle some coarse black pepper onto the surface of an open container of water. Touch the tip of a toothpick into dishwashing liquid, then touch the surface of the water to add the detergent.
  ○ Carefully rest a needle or paper clip on the surface of an open container of water. Push it down with your finger and show the class that it will sink. Retrieve the needle or paper clip and carefully float it on the surface of the water. Tell the students you will sink the object without touching it. Use a dropper to add a few drops of detergent to the water until the paper clip or needle sinks. (It may sink with the addition of the first drop.)

  ○ Carefully rest a paper clip on the surface of a half-full cup of water. Remove the paper clip. Next, bend a paper clip as shown at left and rest it on the surface. Repeat with a full cup whose water level is domed above the rim of the cup. Have students suggest reasons for any observed differences.
  ○ Set a clear glass pie plate on an overhead projector. Fill the pie plate about halfway with water. Cut a circle from a piece of copy paper, heavy paper or index card. Make a spiral as shown in the figure on the next page. (If desired, photocopy the figure onto cardstock or regular office paper. Cut out the spiral along the edge of the dark lines.) Float the spiral on top of the water. Dip a toothpick in dishwashing detergent and touch the toothpick to the water at the center of the spiral and observe.

Spiral Templates

Multiple Images

Enrich the **"Mirror Madness"** *activity in the book* Science Night Family Fun from A to Z *or use as a stand-alone lesson on light, reflection, and mirrors.*

Students use mirrors to make kaleidoscopes.

Key Science Topics

- light
- light reflection
- mirrors

Average Time Required

Setup	20–30	minutes
Performance	20–30	minutes
Cleanup	5	minutes

 **Overview**

· · · · · · · · · · · · · · · # National Science Education Standards

Science as Inquiry Standards

- Abilities Necessary to Do Scientific Inquiry
  Students conduct simple investigations using mirrors.

  Students use their observations to explain how their homemade kaleidoscopes work.

  Students analyze their explanations and those of their classmates during class discussions.

  Students share their observations and explanations with their adult partners and with their classmates.

Physical Science

- Light, Heat, Electricity, and Magnetism
  Light is reflected by a mirror.

- Transfer of Energy
  Light reflected by a mirror enters the eye, allowing us to see the object's reflection.

History and Nature of Science

- Science as a Human Endeavor
  Students investigate how people have used and developed mirrors.

- History of Science
  Students research the history of mirrors in communication.

Science Activity

Materials

3 plastic microscope slides • black electrical tape • 2 black film canisters (1 should have a large circular or triangular hole in the bottom and the other should have a small circular hole in the bottom) • glue stick • 3-inch clear acetate circle • colored acetate, ribbon, confetti, glitter, and similar colorful materials • scissors • straight pin

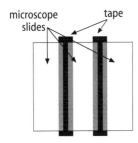

Figure 1

Challenge

Can you use microscope slides to create a kaleidoscope?

Procedure

❶ Place the microscope slides next to one another on a flat surface with their long edges almost touching. Tape the slides together on one side only.

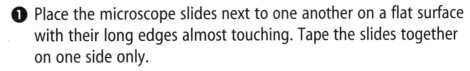

Figure 2

❷ Turn the slides so that the tape side is down as shown in Figure 1. Fold the slides to form a triangle as shown in Figure 2. Tape the two end slides together.

❸ If the film canister is black, go directly to step 4. If the canister is not black, then use tape to completely cover the outside of the slide triangle.

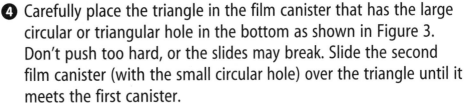

Figure 3

❹ Carefully place the triangle in the film canister that has the large circular or triangular hole in the bottom as shown in Figure 3. Don't push too hard, or the slides may break. Slide the second film canister (with the small circular hole) over the triangle until it meets the first canister.

❺ Tape the two canisters together to make a kaleidoscope as shown in Figure 4. Look through the small circular hole.

❓ *What do you see? What do you think causes these images?*

_____

_____

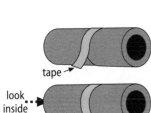

Figure 4

_____

Figure 5

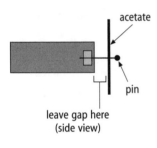

❻ Glue several items onto a 3-inch acetate circle. Try small pieces of colored acetate, ribbon, confetti, glitter, and sequins. (Use scissors to cut out small pieces of acetate and ribbon.) Leave a lot of space between the items.

❼ Push a straight pin through the center of the acetate circle. (See Figure 5.) Tape the pin to the outside of the kaleidoscope so that the acetate circle covers (without touching) the end of the tube with the triangle. Position the acetate circle and the pin so there is a gap between the circle and the tube. (See Figure 6.)

❽ Point the kaleidoscope toward the light, look through the eye hole, and rotate the acetate circle.

? *Describe what you see happening when you rotate the circle.*

_____

_____

_____

❾ If possible, stand with your back to the sun and look through the kaleidoscope. This is really neat to try!

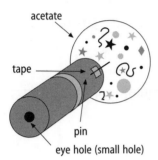

Figure 6

Teacher Notes for the Science Activity

Materials

For Setup only
- hot nail or soldering iron
- utility knife

Per class
- glue stick
- colored acetate, ribbon, confetti, glitter, and sequins

Per student
- 3 plastic microscope slides
- black electrical tape
- 2 black film canisters without lids
- 3-inch clear acetate circle
- scissors
- straight pin

Resources

Plastic microscope slides (#F12899) are available from Frey Scientific, 100 Paragon Parkway, P.O. Box 8101, Mansfield, OH 44901-8101, 800/225-3739.

Setup

- For each student, make a small hole (about 2–3 mm in diameter) in the bottom of one of the film canisters by using a hot nail or soldering iron to melt holes in them. (See Figure 1.)

- Prepare a second film canister for each student by one of the following two methods:

  ○ Method 1 (easier to prepare): Drill a hole approximately ¾ inch in diameter in the bottom of the second film canister (See Figure 2).

  ○ Method 2 (makes a much better kaleidoscope): Using a utility knife, cut a 1.5-cm triangle in the bottom of the second film canister. The triangle should be about the same size as the triangle formed by the three plastic sides when they are in the canister. (See Figure 3.)

Figure 1

Figure 2

Figure 3

Answers and Observations

5 *What do you see? What do you think causes these images?*

Students should see the object reflected many times. The multiple images are caused by light being reflected back and forth between the slides, which act as mirrors.

8 *Describe what you see happening when you rotate the circle.*

They should see multiple images changing as the circle is rotated.

Suggestions for Follow-Up

Have students share their kaleidoscopes with the rest of the class. Discuss what they see when looking through the kaleidoscope and why they see it.

Assessment

Materials

Per class
• object

Per student
• kaleidoscope made in the Science Activity with the acetate circle removed

Challenge

Challenge the students to predict the number of images they will see through their kaleidoscopes (with the decorated acetate circles removed). Hold up an object and have all of the students look at it through their kaleidoscopes. Were they right? Have the students write one important fact or idea they learned during this lesson in their science journals.

Science Explanation

This section explains the science concepts in this lesson as well as in the "Mirror Madness" Family Science Challenge in Science Night Family Fun from A to Z. *It is intended for the teacher's information and may be modified as necessary for discussion with students.*

When you look in a mirror, you see yourself because the mirror reflects the light hitting the mirror. All surfaces reflect light, but not all surfaces function as mirrors. Why does a mirror or other highly polished or smooth surface reflect an image while other surfaces do not? A mirror reflects an image because the incoming parallel light rays from an object remain parallel as they are reflected from the smooth mirror surface. When the reflected light rays reach the eye, they are interpreted by the brain just as if they were reflected from the object itself. The reflection of light rays from a very smooth or polished surface is called regular, or specular, reflection. If the surface is rough, the incoming parallel rays from the object are reflected in all directions. This is called irregular, or diffuse, reflection. This piece of paper is a rough surface, and reflection from this surface is diffuse. Figure 1 illustrates the difference between specular reflection and diffuse reflection.

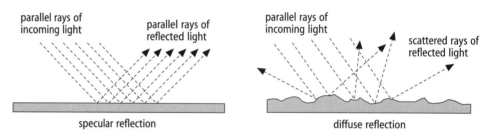

Figure 1

When light hits a mirror or other smooth, polished surface (such as the microscope slides in the classroom Science Activity), it is reflected at the same angle (the angle of reflection) at which it hit the mirror (the angle of incidence). Thus parallel rays of incoming light not only remain parallel when reflected but are reflected at a known angle. (See Figure 2.)

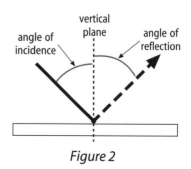

Figure 2

Images in mirrors appear to be behind the mirror. The image appears to be located the same distance behind the mirror as the object is in front of the mirror. This happens because the brain-eye system cannot tell the difference between an object and its reflected image. So the illusion that an object exists behind a mirror results because the light enters the eye exactly as it would have entered if the object were really behind the mirror. (See Figure 3.) The Family Science Challenge explores this illusion.

actual location of reflected object   apparent location of reflected object

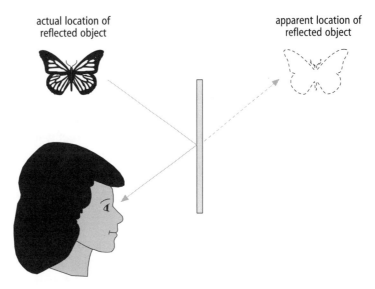

Figure 3

The kaleidoscope in the classroom Science Activity and the Assessment uses the plastic slides with the tape on one side to reflect the incoming light. As light enters the end of the kaleidoscope you see one center image created by light travelling straight down the center. The other images are produced when light reflects off the plastic slides so that three secondary images appear. Upon looking closely, you will see nine additional images. (See Figure 4.)

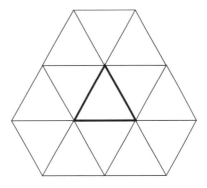

Figure 4

Cross-Curricular Integration

Art and Music

- Have students work with partners to create a mirror dance by matching the movement of their partners. Have each pair practice their dance with music and then perform their dance in front of the class or in small groups.
- Ask students to fold a sheet of paper in half and place a blob of paint on one side. Then, have them fold the other half of the paper over onto the blob of paint. Have students share with the class what they think they have created with their blob of paint.

Language Arts

- Read aloud or have students read the following book:
  - *Reflections,* by Ann Jonas (Greenwillow, ISBN 0688061400)
    A child recalls a perfect day from morning to evening. In each picture, another picture is reflected; halfway through the book the reader turns the book upside down and finishes the story.

Mathematics

- Stand a mirror against one wall in a hallway or room. The wall opposite the mirror should be 6–30 feet away and fairly dark; cover it with a dark cloth or black posterboard if necessary. Sit with a flashlight and face the mirror. Point the flashlight at the mirror but don't turn it on. Hold the flashlight steady. Challenge students to use what they know about how light reflects off a mirror to predict where the flashlight beam will end up after it hits the mirror. Have protractors, metersticks, and string available, but don't hand them out until students ask for them or need a hint. You may also wish to remind them that light reflects off the mirror at the same angle at which it hits the mirror. Have students write their names on pieces of masking tape and place the tape on the wall where they think the flashlight beam will hit. Turn on the flashlight and see where it lands on the opposite wall. Move to the left or the right to change the angle of the flashlight and repeat the experiment a few more times.

Social Studies

- Research and discuss with students the use of mirrors in carnival fun houses.
- Research and discuss the use of mirrors as communication devices.

Just for Fun

- Ask students to use a mirror to write a secret message and give it to a friend, who can read the message using another mirror.
- Have students print their whole names in large capital letters on a piece of paper. Give them a small mirror and tell them to move the mirror above and next to each letter, looking for any "mirror twins."
- Show the Marx Brothers movie "Duck Soup," which contains a famous mirror scene with Harpo dressed as Groucho.

No-Leak Novelties

Enrich the **"Nifty Balloon Trick"** *activity in the book* Science Night Family Fun from A to Z *or use as a stand-alone lesson on gas pressure and polymers.*

Students investigate astonishing things they can do with balloons, pennies, and water-filled plastic bags.

.... **Key Science Topics**

- gas pressure
- polymers and their properties

.... **Average Time Required**

Setup	5	minutes
Performance	10	minutes
Cleanup	5	minutes

············ # National Science Education Standards

Science as Inquiry Standards

- Abilities Necessary to Do Scientific Inquiry
  Students investigate the behavior of a balloon and a plastic bag.

  Students use their observation of the behavior of the balloon and plastic bag to propose a reasonable explanation for it.

  Students use their observations to develop cause-and-effect relationships about how a skewered balloon, a penny in a balloon with a hole, and a punctured plastic bag behave.

  Students share their observations and explanations with their families and classmates.

Physical Science

- Properties of Objects and Materials
  Balloons have many observable properties.

  Balloons can be described by the properties of the polymers from which they are made.

- Position and Motion of Objects
  Air moves out of the balloon when the skewer is removed.

- Motions and Forces
  Pressure forces hold the penny in place over the hole in the balloon despite the motion of the balloon.

History and Nature of Science

- Science as a Human Endeavor
  Students learn how people from many cultures discovered and developed the use of latex.

  Students learn how scientists have improved natural latex.

- History of Science
  Students learn about the history of latex and how people have used latex for many years.

Science Activity

Materials

penny • balloon • bamboo skewer or sharpened pencil • cooking oil • scissors • zipper-type plastic bag • water • sharpened pencil • sink, tub, or basin

Challenge

Can you poke a hole in a container without spilling the contents?

Procedure

Skewers and sharpened pencils should be handled with care; hold the balloons away from people's faces, as the balloons may pop. If you or someone on your team is allergic to latex, do not have that person handle the balloon in this activity.

Part A

❶ Place a penny inside a balloon, then inflate the balloon to half its intended size and tie it off.

❷ Dip the tip of the skewer or tip of the sharpened pencil into the cooking oil. Use your finger to spread the oil over the bottom 1 inch of the skewer or pencil.

❸ To make a hole in the balloon without popping it, find the thickest part of the rubber at the center bottom of the balloon at the end opposite the tie end. (See Figure 1.) Slowly twist and push the skewer or pencil through this part of the balloon. Then remove the skewer or pencil and quickly cover the hole with your finger.

Figure 1

❹ Turn the balloon so that the penny covers the hole inside the balloon. Remove your finger from the hole. Move the balloon around.

? *What happens to the penny?*

_____

_____

_____

5 Set the balloon aside for 10–15 minutes. Then look at it again.

? *Is the balloon still inflated? Explain why you think this happens.*

_____

_____

_____

6 Poke a second hole in the thick part of the balloon at the tied end.

? *What happens to the penny? What happens to the balloon?*

_____

_____

_____

7 Cut the balloon open and retrieve the penny.

Part B

1 Fill a zipper-type plastic bag about two-thirds full with water and seal the bag.

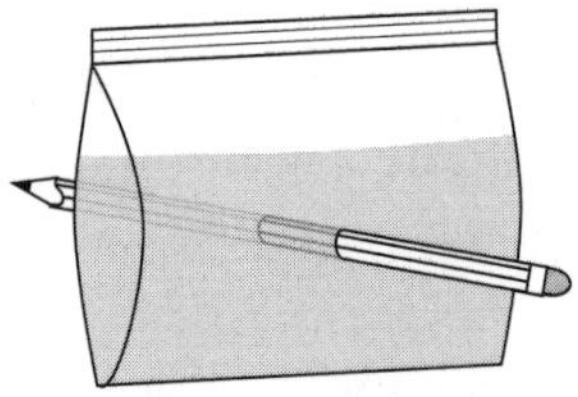

2 Carefully, yet firmly and quickly, poke a sharpened pencil all the way through so that it protrudes from both sides as shown in Figure 2. *(Helpful tip: Do this activity over a sink, tub, or basin just in case the seal on the plastic bag opens or the pencil is pulled out of the bag.)*

Figure 2

? *Describe what happens.*

_____

_____

_____

Teacher Notes for the Science Activity

Materials

Per class, per student, or per group
- penny
- balloon
- bamboo skewer or sharpened pencil
- cooking oil
- scissors
- zipper-type plastic bag
- water
- sharpened pencil
- sink, tub, or basin
- (optional) paper towels

Resources

Latex balloons can be purchased from a florist's shop, department store, magic store, or balloon store. The balloons should not be too old. Round balloons work better than sausage-shaped balloons because they are less likely to pop. If large quantities are required, balloons may be purchased from National Latex Products, 246 E. 4th St., Ashland, OH 44805, 419/289-3300. A minimum order is required for mail orders.

Answers and Observations

Part A

❹ *What happens to the penny?*

The penny "sticks" to the balloon at the hole even when the balloon is turned so that the penny is at the top of the balloon.

❺ *Is the balloon still inflated? Explain why you think this happens.*

The balloon is probably still inflated. The penny seals the hole in the balloon and the air does not escape.

❻ *What happens to the penny? What happens to the balloon?*

The penny stays in place, but the balloon deflates.

Part B

❷ *Describe what happens.*

The pencil goes through the bag, but the water does not leak out.

Suggestions for Follow-Up

Have students discuss their observations and possible reasons for them. Have students consider how and why the balloon and plastic bag act similarly.

References

"Needle Through a Balloon"; *Fun With Chemistry: A Guidebook of K–12 Activities;* Sarquis, M., Sarquis, J., Eds.; Institute for Chemical Education: Madison, WI, 1991; Vol. 1, pp 139–142.

Toepker, T., Department of Physics, Xavier University, Cincinnati, OH, personal communication.

Woodward, L. "Skewering a Balloon," *Polymers All Around You!;* Terrific Science: Middletown, OH, 1992; p 18.

Assessment

Materials

Per student
- 1 or both of the following sets of materials:
  - several different kinds of zipper-type plastic bags (freezer, sandwich, regular, snack, etc.), several sharpened pencils, and water
  - several balloons, several pennies, and cooking oil

Challenge

Challenge students to design experiments to determine 1) which kind of zipper-type plastic bag will remain leak-proof with the most pencils stuck through it and/or 2) how many pennies they can stick to the inside of a balloon as in Part A. Have students write or discuss a plan for their experiment that includes filling several different kinds of bags with water, sealing them, and piercing them with pencils, or filling balloons to equal sizes, adding pennies, and poking holes of equal size. Instruct them to carry out the experiment and record their observations. Hold a class discussion on what the findings were. End by having the students write one important fact or idea they learned in this lesson in their science journals.

Depending on the age of the students, you may want to discuss the problem of controls in this type of experiment. Some of the factors that might need to be controlled in order for the results to be compared in a meaningful manner are
- similarities in the shape, style, dimension, and sharpness of the pencils used;
- the height and mass of the water in the bags;
- consistency of the method and location of the pencil insertion; and/or
- the size of the inflated balloons.

Science Explanation

This section explains the science concepts in this lesson as well as in the "Nifty Balloon Trick" Family Science Challenge in Science Night Family Fun from A to Z. *It is intended for the teacher's information and may be modified as necessary for discussion with students.*

Balloons are made by dipping a mold, called a mandrel, into a vat of liquid latex (natural rubber) and then pulling the mold out again so that a thin film of material is left adhering to it. (This process is called dip coating.) The thin sheet of latex that is formed contains many long intertwined polymer chains. The elasticity of these polymer chains causes latex to be stretchy. Blowing up the balloon stretches these polymer chains. As shown in the figure below, the strands in the middle region of the balloon stretch more than the regions at the tie and at the nipple end (opposite the tie), which are thicker due to the molding process.

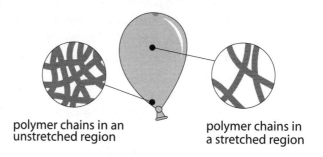

polymer chains in an
unstretched region

polymer chains in
a stretched region

In the Family Science Challenge, families discovered that when a sharp, lubricated skewer pierces the thick ends of the latex balloon, the polymer strands that make up the latex are gently pushed aside. When the skewer is removed, the air can be felt leaking out through the holes where the strands were pushed apart. The balloon will deflate slowly, not burst suddenly. It is necessary to use a smooth, sharp skewer for this activity. A dull skewer is more likely to tear the polymer chains.

When the balloon is given a quick jab to its side with the skewer, it pops. The latex is thin and the polymer chains are tightly stretched at the sides of the balloon and are unable to slide apart any further without tearing. Once a tear begins, it rapidly continues as the air rushes out, causing the balloon to pop.

The cooking oil that is spread on the skewer acts as a lubricant and also partially blocks the hole, slowing the escape rate of air. Lubricants are liquids that help matter move more smoothly. In this experiment, the cooking oil coats the skewer and makes it more slippery, allowing it to slide through the latex more easily. Most machines and vehicles with moving parts need lubricants. For example, bicycles use bicycle grease to help the chains move more smoothly over the gears, and car engines need oil to lubricate the pistons and valves inside.

In the classroom Science Activity, students observe that when the balloon with the penny inside is skewered and the skewer is removed, air begins to leak out. This is because the air pressure inside the balloon is greater than the air pressure outside the balloon. (Think about how hard you have to blow to fill the balloon.) When the penny is moved over the hole, it blocks the air and keeps it from escaping. The higher air pressure inside the balloon pushes the penny against the hole and keeps it there. This situation is similar to that of a suction cup, except that with the suction cup the greater pressure is on the outside. If the penny is forced away from the hole, air will once again escape and the penny will move independently of the balloon.

In the Science Activity and Assessment, the pencil through the plastic bag works like the skewer through the balloon. The pencil pushes the polymer strands out of the way over an area just the size of a cross-section of the pencil. The elasticity of the bag pushes these strands back against the sides of the pencil, sealing the bag and keeping the water trapped inside. When the pencil is removed, the strands will not completely return to their original positions, so water will flow out the holes.

Cross-Curricular Integration

Language Arts

- Write a concrete poem in the shape of a balloon, filling the balloon with concepts related to the activity.

Social Studies

- Have students investigate the sources of natural latex and the history of its use.

Just for Fun

- Blow up a balloon but do NOT tie it off. Write a message on the inflated balloon with a permanent marker. Deflate the balloon. Challenge others to figure out the message without blowing up the balloon. Then blow it up and watch the message emerge as it stretches.
- Invite a magician to teach the class several "magic tricks" and explain the science behind them.
- Construct various figures (such as animals) using balloons.

Optical Oddities

Enrich the **"Optical Illusions"** *activity in the book* Science Night Family Fun from A to Z *or use as a stand-alone lesson on persistence of vision and other optical illusions.*

Is seeing always believing? No! Students will study some optical illusions and discover that what they see is not always what is there.

Key Science Topics

- persistence of vision
- sight

Average Time Required

Science Activity 1

Setup	5–10 minutes
Performance	15–20 minutes
Cleanup	5 minutes

Science Activity 2

Setup	5–10 minutes
Performance	10–15 minutes
Cleanup	5 minutes

National Science Education Standards

Science as Inquiry Standards:

- Abilities Necessary to Do Scientific Inquiry
  Students investigate various types of optical illusions.

  Students share their observations with the class and together construct explanations for their observations.

Physical Science

- Properties of Objects and Materials
  The eye retains images briefly through a phenomenon called persistence of vision.

- Transfer of Energy
  Light is scattered by objects and enters the eye, allowing the objects to be seen.

Life Science

- Structure and Function in Living Systems
  Specialized cells in the eye that react with light cause images to be retained, a phenomenon called persistence of vision.

History and Nature of Science

- Science as a Human Endeavor
  Students learn how people from different cultures used the phenomenon of persistence of vision to create games, puzzles, movies, and other objects.

- History of Science
  Students learn how the phenomenon of persistence of vision has been used throughout history.

Science Activity 1

Materials

Divided Circle pattern • scissors • set of crayons or colored pencils • piece of cardboard • tape • nail or large pin • short pencil • 2 rubber bands • Blank Circle Pattern

Challenge

Can you use persistence of vision to mix colors?

Procedure

❶ Cut out the Divided Circle pattern.

❷ Lightly color each of the divisions in the circle with its corresponding color starting with red (R) and continuing with orange (O), yellow (Y), green (G), blue (B), and purple (P).

❸ Trace the Divided Circle pattern onto the cardboard and cut out the cardboard circle. Tape the Divided Circle pattern onto the cardboard circle.

❹ Carefully poke a small hole in the center of the circle using the nail or pin.

❺ Push the pointed end of the pencil through the hole on the front of the Divided Circle pattern. (The colored side should face away from the pencil point.) Slide the cardboard circle to just above the taper of the pencil point.

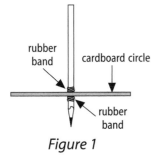

rubber band

cardboard circle

rubber band

Figure 1

❻ Wrap one rubber band around the pencil above the cardboard circle and a second rubber band below the circle. (See Figure 1.) Your spinner is ready to test.

❼ Spin the spinner like a top, with the point of the pencil down. If the spinner doesn't spin quickly and smoothly, try adjusting the location of the cardboard circle on the pencil. The circle must be flat and parallel to the table for it to spin. Practice until you can spin the spinner quickly and smoothly.

? *What color is the paper circle when the spinner is spinning quickly and smoothly?*

_____

❽ Cut out the Blank Circle pattern and draw a design on it. Poke out the hole in the center, and lightly tape it on top of the Divided Circle pattern on the spinner.

? *What do you think will happen to the design when you spin the spinner?*

_____

_____

❾ Spin the spinner.

? *Describe what you see and draw a picture below.*

_____

_____

_____

_____

Science Activity 2

Materials

ruler

Challenge

Can you see the optical illusions?

Procedure

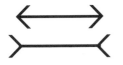

Figure 1

❶ Look carefully at the two drawings in Figure 1.

? *Each drawing contains a horizontal line. From your observations, are the horizontal lines the same length, or are they different lengths?*

_____

❷ Now measure the straight portion of each of the lines in Figure 1 with the ruler.

? *Are they the same length, or are they different lengths?*

_____

Figure 2

❸ Look at the horizontal lines in Figure 2.

? *Do the horizontal lines appear to be the same length or different lengths?*

_____

❹ Use the ruler to measure the horizontal lines.

? *Are the horizontal lines the same length, or are they different lengths?*

_____

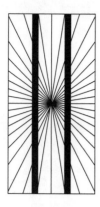

Figure 3

5 Look at the two heavy lines down the middle of Figure 3.

? *Do these two thick lines look straight, or do they look bent?*

_____

6 Line up your ruler with one of the thick lines on the drawing.

? *Are the two thick lines straight, or are they bent?*

_____

Teacher Notes for Science Activity 1

Materials

For Setup only
• scissors or paper cutter

Per student or group
• Divided Circle pattern (provided)
• scissors
• set of crayons or colored pencils
• piece of thin (not corrugated) cardboard

> *Cardboard from a cereal box works well.*

• tape
• nail or large pin
• short pencil about 3 inches long

> *Golf pencils work well for this activity. You can also use old, sharpened-down pencils.*

• 2 rubber bands
• Blank Circle pattern

Setup

Photocopy the Divided and Blank Circles patterns. Use a paper cutter or scissors to cut apart the patterns into rectangles. You can let students cut out the individual circles if you wish, or you can do it yourself.

Answers and Observations

❼ *What color is the paper circle when the spinner is spinning quickly and smoothly?*

The circle will probably appear to be a "creamy" color. If the disk had seven sections and indigo and violet were included, the disk would appear to be white.

Suggestions for Follow-Up

White light is a combination of different colors of light. One combination that gives white light is the rainbow colors: red, orange, yellow, green, blue, indigo, and violet. Discuss how this combination of colors along with persistence of vision makes the spinning disk look all one color.

As a class, compare the designs students drew on the Blank Circle. Which look the best when spinning? Why? Have students make one or two more designs on fresh Blank Circle patterns and see what happens when they are spun.

Teacher Notes for Science Activity 2

Materials

Per student
• ruler

Answers and Observations

❶ *Each drawing contains a horizontal line. From your observations, are the horizontal lines the same length, or are they different lengths?*

The straight portions of the drawings appear to most people to be different lengths.

❷ *Are they the same length, or are they different lengths?*

The horizontal portions of the lines are the same length.

❸ *Do the horizontal lines appear to be the same length or different lengths?*

To most people, the horizontal lines appear to be different lengths.

❹ *Are the horizontal lines the same length, or are they different lengths?*

The horizontal lines are the same length.

❺ *Do these two thick lines look straight, or do they look bent?*

The two thick lines look bent to most people.

❻ *Are the two thick lines straight, or are they bent?*

The two thick lines are straight.

Suggestions for Follow-Up

As a class, compare students' observations in steps 1, 3, and 5. Did they see optical illusions? Ask students how they think these illusions are produced.

Classroom Science from Ⓐ to Ⓩ

Assessment

Materials

Per student
- spinner made in Science Activity 1
- Swirl pattern (provided)
- Concentric Circles pattern (provided)
- crayons or colored pencils

Setup

Photocopy the Swirls and Concentric Circles pattern. Use a paper cutter or scissors to cut apart the patterns into rectangles. You can let students cut out the individual circles if you wish, or you can do it yourself.

Challenge

Have students cut out the Swirl pattern and the Concentric Circle pattern. They should then color only the thin areas of each of these patterns and leave the thicker parts uncolored. For the swirl pattern, this will result in the thin swirl being colored and the thick part uncolored. For the concentric circle pattern, this will result in four thin circles that are colored, with an uncolored thick circle between each. Note that the circle closest to the center should remain uncolored also. (See Figure 1.) Once the cutting and coloring is completed, have students predict what the spinning patterns will look like and then test their predictions.

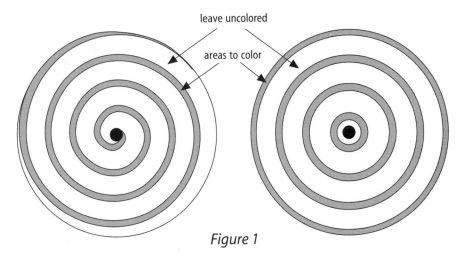

Figure 1

Discuss observations as a class. Which circle gave a new pattern when spun, and why? Have students write one important fact or idea they learned during this lesson in their science journals.

Science Explanation

This section explains the science concepts in this lesson as well as in the "Optical Illusions" Family Science Challenge in Science Night Family Fun from A to Z. *It is intended for the teacher's information and may be modified as necessary for discussion with students.*

In the Family Science Challenge, the illusion that the pictures on both sides of the thaumatrope are a single picture (as well as the illusion of motion in movies, animated cartoons, and flip books) is caused by a phenomenon called persistence of vision. The retina of the eye contains an enormous number of molecules of a substance called retinal, which can exist in either of two forms, "cis" or "trans." Reflected light from one side of the thaumatrope disk hits the cis-retinal molecules in one area of the retina, quickly converting them to trans-retinal and triggering the brain to form an image of that side of the thaumatrope. The trans-retinal form lingers for about $\frac{1}{15}$ second, causing the image to remain even after the disk turns to the other side when it is spinning quickly. Reflected light from the other side of the disk hits a different part of the retina, repeating the process. The persistence of one image while another appears creates the illusion seen when the thaumatrope is turned.

White light can be split into many colors, as seen in a rainbow or with a prism. Likewise, many colors of light can be combined to make white light. The colors on the spinner in Science Activity 1 are combined because of persistence of vision. The color produced by the combination will be close to white (but not pure white because the colors used are not the exact combination needed for white).

In Science Activity 2, students investigate other kinds of optical illusions besides those produced by persistence of vision. The illusions in this activity occur when our brains do not accurately interpret what we see.

In the Assessment, students revisit the phenomenon of persistence of vision. The swirl pattern seems to move as it spins, while the concentric circles exhibit no visible change due to their regular, symmetrical pattern.

Cross-Curricular Integration

Art and Music

- Bring in pictures by M.C. Escher to share with the class. Many M.C. Escher books are available, including *The Graphic Work of M.C. Escher* (Wing, ISBN 0517385732), *M.C. Escher: His Life and Complete Graphic Work* (Harry N. Abrams, ISBN 0810981130), and *The Pop-Up Book of M.C. Escher* (Pomegranate, ISBN 0876548192).
- Share other books involving optical illusions with students, including *Visual Foolery*, by Michael DiSpezio (Tormont, ISBN 2-7641-0213-5). This book features mind benders, eye poppers, optical illusions, 3-D images, and other visual tricks. Includes 3-D glasses, two pencils, one flip book, and different cards.
- Show students several examples of stereograms, three-dimensional illusions commonly marketed as Magic Eye® pictures. These images are available in books and calendars, and sometimes in comic-strip form. You may also want to visit the web site of Magic Eye, Inc., a producer of stereogram images, at www.magiceye.com
- Investigate early movie- and cartoon-making techniques. How did artists integrate motion into their work to produce movies and cartoons?
- Bring in flip books for students to observe. (Some page-a-day calendars also have small images in one corner that appear to move when the calendar is flipped through rapidly.) Examples include *Ed Emberley's 3 Science Flip Books*, by Ed Emberley (Little, Brown, ISBN 0-316-23456-7), a set of three books featuring six nature adventures.
- Show video clips where persistence of vision has strange effects, such as causing wagon wheels to appear to turn backward.

Language Arts

- Write a poem about the idea that seeing is not always believing.
- Read aloud or have students read the following book:
  - *Carousel,* by Donald Crews (Greenwillow, ISBN 0688009085)
    The full-color illustrations in this book show what happens to the brightly colored carousel horses as a merry-go-round starts, speeds up, and slows down.

Mathematics

- Challenge students to draw optical illusions or tilings like those of M.C. Escher, which use many mathematical concepts, including symmetry. The artist M.C. Escher studied mathematics to improve his own artwork. (See the Art and Music section.) One such optical illusion is the cube shown at the right. Is it sitting level or is it tilted? Other classic illusions involve stacks of cubes and pictures that look like one thing or another, depending on your perspective.

Social Studies

- Have students research how pre-movie news reels (the reels that were shown in theaters before feature films) changed how Americans learned of events going on at home and around the world, especially during World Wars I and II. Encourage students to interview grandparents or other older family members who may have been around when news reels were used before movies.

Divided and Blank Circles

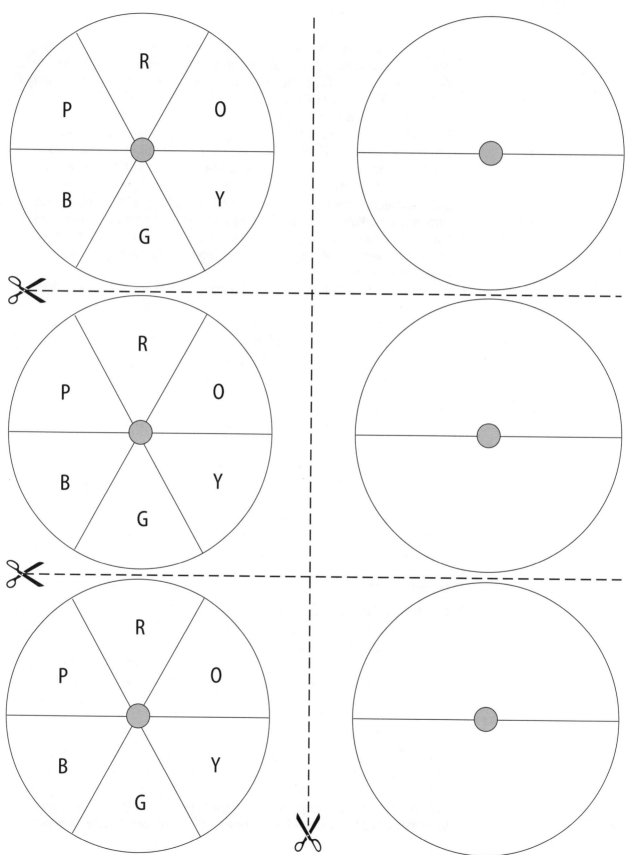

Swirls and Concentric Circles

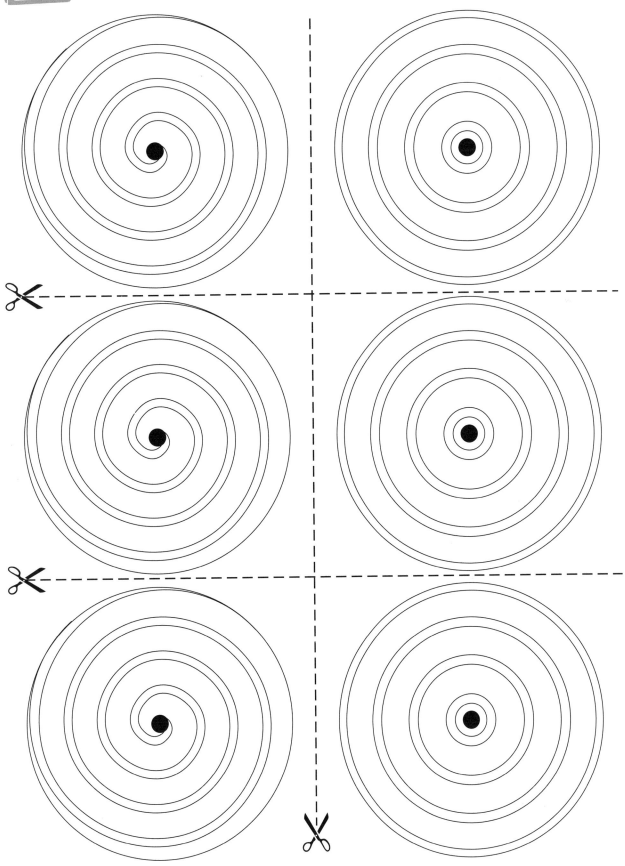

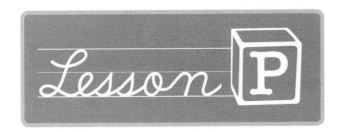

Playful Bubbles

*Enrich the **"Popping Patterns"** activity in the book* Science Night Family Fun from A to Z *or use as a stand-alone lesson on bubbles.*

Students look at the relationship between different bubble blowers and the bubbles they produce.

. . . . **Key Science Topics**

- color
- light
- reflection
- constructive and destructive interference
- soap bubbles
- waves

. . . . **Average Time Required**

Setup	15 minutes
Performance	35 minutes
Cleanup	15 minutes

.... National Science Education Standards
Science as Inquiry Standards

- Abilities Necessary to Do Scientific Inquiry
  Students question how many soap solution "window panes" will be created after a three-dimensional shape is dipped in the soap solution.

  Students investigate and use their observations to verify their predictions about the window pane.

  Students investigate the colors of soap bubbles in the Family Science Challenge.

  Students use their observations during the Family Science Challenge to determine the color of soap bubbles immediately before they pop.

  Students investigate the impact of the size and shape of bubble blowers on the bubbles produced.

  Students share their observations with their adult partners and their classmates.

Physical Science

- Properties of Objects and Materials
  Soap bubbles floating in air are almost spherical in shape despite the shape of the bubble blower.

- Motions and Forces
  Gravity pulls the soap solution of a bubble from the top of the bubble to the bottom, which causes the thickness of the bubble wall to change.

- Light, Heat, Electricity, and Magnetism
  Light travels in a straight line until it hits and is reflected by both the outside and inside surfaces of a soap bubble.

Science Activity

Materials

potato pieces • toothpicks • bubble solution in a plastic bowl

Challenge

What kind of bubble windows can be made with three dimensional (3-D) shapes?

Procedure

❶ Using the potato pieces and toothpicks provided, build a square. A square is a two-dimensional object that has only one side. Scientists sometimes call this side a "face."

❷ Dip the square completely into the bubble solution. When you pull it out, carefully observe the bubble film that is created. We will call this bubble film a window pane.

❸ Now look at Table 1. You will see the information on the square is already recorded. You will complete the rest of the chart as you make, examine, and dip the remaining objects.

❹ Build a cube. A cube is a three-dimensional object. How many faces does the cube have? Record this number in Observation Table 1.

❺ Predict the number of window panes that will be created by dipping the shape into the bubble solution. Write your prediction in the table. Then dip your cube completely into the bubble solution and count and record the number of window panes that are actually created.

❻ Make the tetrahedron and one other three-dimensional shape of your choosing. Repeat the procedure with both of these shapes and record the information requested in Observation Table 1.

Observation Table 1

Shapes	square	cube	tetrahedron	
Number of Faces (Sides)	1			
Predicted Number of Soap Film Window Panes	1			
Actual Number of Window Panes	1			

❼ Use the four shapes you made as bubble blowers. Dip each shape in the soap solution, then blow into it to determine the shape of the bubble that is produced. Record your findings in Observation Table 2.

Observation Table 2

Bubble Blower Shape		Description of Bubble
square		
cube		
tetrahedron		

Teacher Notes
for the Science Activity

triangular prism
6 faces

cube
6 faces

rectangular prism
6 faces

square pyramid
5 faces

tetrahedron
4 faces

octahedron
8 faces

trigonal bipyramid
6 faces

Materials

Per class
- bubble solution made from the following:
  - 1 gallon water
  - ⅔ cup Dawn or Joy® dishwashing liquid
  - (optional) 1 tablespoon glycerin
- container to mix and store solution in

Per student
- toothpicks
- potato pieces
- plastic bowl

Safety

The soap solution is slippery. Wipe up any spilled solution immediately. Vinegar is helpful in cleaning up soap spills.

Setup

Make the bubble solution by combining the required amounts of water, dishwashing liquid, and glycerin. For best results, make this solution several hours to several days in advance and let it sit. Aging tends to result in better bubbles.

Tip

Many three-dimensional shapes can easily be made with the toothpicks and potato pieces. Some examples are shown at left.

Suggestion for Follow-Up

Have the class discuss how the sizes and shapes of the bubble blowers affect the bubbles produced.

Reference

Barber, J., et al. "Bubble Technology"; *Bubbleology,* Great Explorations in Math and Science (GEMS); Lawrence Hall of Science: Berkeley, CA, 1986; pp 5–9.

Assessment

Materials

Per class or per group
- bubble solution made from the following:
  - 1 gallon water
  - ⅔ cup Dawn or Joy® dishwashing liquid
  - (optional) 1 tablespoon glycerin
- container to mix and store solution in
- commercial bubble-blowing wands and loops
- common household items to make bubble blowers, such as:
  - 4–5 metal cans of the same diameter with both ends removed and all rims taped
  - coffee can with both ends removed and rims taped
  - funnel
  - basting bulb
  - cardboard tubes
  - paper
- paper towels
- large, shallow tray
- duct tape or masking tape (if necessary)

Resources

Pre-made bubble solution, with commercial bubble wands and loops, is available at toy stores and discount department stores.

Safety

If metal cans are used as bubble blowers, tape the rim of each opening so that no sharp edges are exposed. The soap solution is slippery. Wipe up any spilled solution immediately. You may want to do this activity outside to prevent messes.

Setup

- Make the bubble solution by combining the water, dishwashing liquid, and glycerin. For best results, make this solution several hours to several days in advance and let it sit. Aging tends to result in better bubbles.
- Pour some bubble solution into the shallow tray.

Challenge

Challenge students to determine which common household items are able to make the largest bubble and which can make the most bubbles at once. Tell students to use both words and pictures to describe what they did in their science journals.

Suggestions for Follow-Up

What kind of bubble does each bubble blower make? How do the size and shape of the blower affect the bubbles? *The longer the tube, the stronger the bubble, because the air flow into the bubble is smoother. Wider-mouthed bubble blowers generally produce bigger bubbles.* After this discussion, have students write one important fact or idea they learned in this lesson in their science journals.

Science Explanation

This section explains the science concepts in this lesson as well as in the "Popping Patterns" Family Science Challenge in Science Night Family Fun from A to Z. *It is intended for the teacher's information and may be modified as necessary for discussion with students.*

During the Family Science Challenge, families will probably discover a repeating color sequence similar to the following: green, blue, magenta (or pink), yellow, green, blue, magenta, yellow, white, white with black spots, and black. Then the bubble pops. These color changes are caused by the soap bubble film's becoming thinner. (See Figure 1.) In cases where absolutely no air disturbances are present, such as in a vacuum, scientists have reported seeing this pattern. Air currents interfere with the thinning of the bubble wall and interrupt the usual pattern of colors, so not all participants may see the pattern in its entirety. Even if air disturbances are present, however, participants may see portions of this sequence.

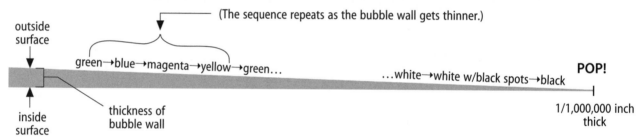

Figure 1

The colors on the bubble are caused by waves of light reflecting off the bubble surfaces. White light contains waves of many different colors of light. Each wave is made up of two parts: a crest (the highest part of the wave) and a trough (the lowest part of the wave). (See Figure 2.) The length of a wave from crest to crest (wavelength) determines its color. Violet light has the shortest wavelength of the visible light waves, and red has the longest. When light hits the bubble, some waves of each color of light are reflected by the outer surface of the bubble wall, and some waves pass through the wall and are reflected by the inner surface.

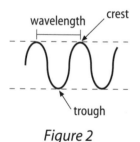

Figure 2

When the thickness of the bubble wall is such that the two reflected parts of one color of wave (the one reflected from the outer surface and the one reflected from the inner surface) leave the bubble in step, crest to crest, that color appears brighter. (See Figure 3a.) This is called constructive interference. Sometimes the two reflected parts of one color of wave will emerge out of step, crest to trough, canceling each other out, and this color will not be seen. (See Figure 3b.) This is called destructive interference.

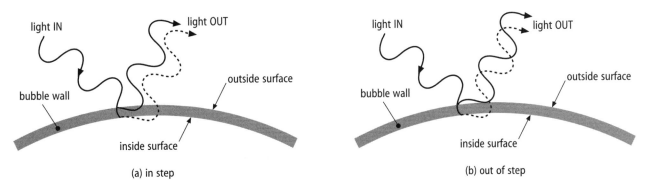

Figure 3

As the wall gets thinner, the waves that interfere constructively and destructively change, resulting in the changing colors.

When the wall is less than ¼ of a wavelength thick for any color, none of the colors are completely canceled, and the bubble appears white. Black spots appear when the wall is super-thin—about one-millionth of an inch thick. This occurs because light reflected from the outer surface is always reversed (all troughs become crests), but the light reflected from the inner surface is not reversed. Thus, when the wall is super-thin, every color of light wave will cancel itself and no light will be seen. The bubble is transparent, allowing the color of the black paper underneath to show through.

In the classroom Science Activity and the Assessment, students will find that the shape of a single bubble will always be a sphere once it is released from a blower. Most items with round openings work well as bubble blowers. Those with longer tubes generally produce stronger bubbles because air currents are blocked out, making the flow of air into the bubble smoother.

Cross-Curricular Integration

Art and Music

- Pour a small amount of tempera paint on top of a tray of water. Have students use a straw to blow bubbles in the paint. Instruct students to carefully lay a piece of white paper on the paint bubbles, then slowly pull it off. The paint bubbles will leave a design on the paper.

Language Arts

- Read aloud or have students read one or more of the following books:
  - *A Drop of Water,* by Walter Wick (Scholastic, ISBN 0-590-22197-3)
    This book of photographs includes many pictures of bubbles.
  - *The Magic Bubble Trip,* by Ingrid and Dieter Schubert (Kane/Miller, ISBN 0916291030)
    James blows a giant bubble that carries him away to a land of large, hairy frogs.

Mathematics

- Measure the time it takes a bubble dome to pop. Repeat for several trials. Find the average of these times, then create a few more bubbles and time how long they take to pop. How many pop before the average time? How many pop after the average time?
- Try using different detergents with and without glycerin. Compare the popping times by constructing bar graphs.
- Measure the circumferences of the bubble domes. Bubbles will often leave a distinct "ring" on the surface after they pop. Measuring this ring with a piece of string or measuring tape will give students a good estimate of the circumference of the bubble.
- Discuss the relationship between the volume and the surface area for different three-dimensional shapes. Relate these findings to the reason bubbles are spherical.

Just for Fun

- Make giant bubbles outside using a hula hoop or other large hoop and a "kiddie" pool about half-full with bubble solution. To make a bubble column with a hula hoop, place the hula hoop in the pool. Place a sturdy step stool inside the pool. Make sure the top of the stool is not submerged in the solution. Have a student step carefully onto the stool. Have five or six students lift the hula hoop carefully, creating a bubble column surrounding the student on the stool.

Quirky Quills

Enrich the **"Quaint Paint"** *activity in the book* Science Night Family Fun from A to Z *or use as a stand-alone lesson on solubility.*

Students investigate the solubility of permanent and water-soluble markers in two different solvents.

Key Science Topics

- solubility
- solvents

Average Time Required

Setup	5	minutes
Performance	10–20	minutes plus drying time
Cleanup	5	minutes

. . . . **National Science Education Standards**
Science as Inquiry Standards

*   Abilities Necessary to Do Scientific Inquiry
    Students predict whether or not colored dyes (from permanent and water-soluble markers and "Paint with Water" pages) will dissolve in different solvents (water, isopropyl alcohol, oil, etc.).

    Students conduct simple experiments to test their predictions.

    Students use magnifying lenses to make careful observations of their experimental results.

    Students identify whether visible changes were the result of the dissolving process or of chromatography and use their previous observations to develop explanations to justify their choices.

    Students share the results of their investigations with their adult partners and with other students. This includes both written observations and participation in discussions.

Physical Science

*   Properties of Objects and Materials
    Materials, including inks, have many observable properties, such as whether or not they will dissolve in certain substances.

    Inks can be divided into categories by their properties including solubility. For example, inks may be water-soluble or permanent (not water-soluble).

History and Nature of Science

*   History of Science
    Students learn about the history of dyes and inks and how they have been developed for use in different cultures.

Science Activity

Materials

2 sheets of 8½-inch x 11-inch paper • water-soluble marker
• permanent marker • pencil • 2 small paintbrushes • container of
water • container of isopropyl alcohol (91% or greater)

Challenge

Can you create your own Paint with Water picture?

Procedure

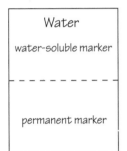

Figure 1

Figure 2

❶ Fold the two sheets of paper in half horizontally and open them both up. Use a water-soluble marker to write the words "water-soluble marker" on the top halves of both sheets of paper, as shown in Figures 1 and 2.

❷ Use a permanent marker to write the words "permanent marker" on the bottom halves of both sheets of paper, as shown in Figures 1 and 2.

❸ Use a pencil to write the word "water" at the very top of one sheet of paper (as shown in Figure 1) and the words "isopropyl alcohol" at the very top of the other sheet of paper (as shown in Figure 2).

❹ Use a small paintbrush to paint water all over the sheet of paper you labeled "water." Be sure to paint over all of the words.

? *What do you observe?*

_____

_____

_____

5 Use a different small paintbrush to paint isopropyl alcohol all over the sheet of paper you labeled "isopropyl alcohol." Be sure to go over all of the words (both the ones in ink and the ones in pencil) as if you were painting over them.

? *What do you observe?*

_____

_____

_____

6 Use what you learned to create your own Paint with Water picture on a new sheet of paper. Write instructions for a friend to follow to "color" your picture.

Teacher Notes
for the Science Activity

Materials

Per student
- 2 half sheets of 8½-inch x 11-inch paper
- water-soluble marker
- permanent marker
- pencil
- 2 small paintbrushes
- container of water
- container of isopropyl alcohol (91% or greater)

Resources

The 91% isopropyl alcohol used in this activity is 91% isopropyl alcohol and 9% water and can be purchased at drug stores. Do not use rubbing alcohol, which is 70% isopropyl alcohol and 30% water.

Safety

Isopropyl alcohol is intended for external use only; avoid ingestion or contact with eyes. Do not do this activity near an open flame.

Disposal

Unused alcohol can be saved or flushed down the drain with water.

Answers and Observations

❹ *What do you observe?*

The water dissolves some of the water-soluble ink but does not dissolve the ink from the permanent marker.

❺ *What do you observe?*

The isopropyl alcohol dissolves some of the permanent-marker ink and some of the water-soluble ink.

Suggestion for Follow-Up

Have the class discuss their observations and what they can conclude about which ink is soluble in water and which is soluble in isopropyl alcohol.

Reference

Sarquis, M.; Sarquis, J.L.; Williams, J.P. "Paint with Water Books"; *Teaching Chemistry with TOYS: Activities for Grades K–9;* McGraw-Hill: New York, 1995; pp 87–92.

Student Assessment

Materials

2 pieces of white cloth • coffee can or butter tub with plastic lid with large hole in center • permanent marker • water-soluble marker • dropper • small cup of water • small cup of isopropyl alcohol

Procedure

Part 1: Water Test

Figure 1

❶ Stretch one piece of white fabric over the opening of the coffee can or butter tub and hold it in place while putting the plastic lid on the can or tub as shown in Figure 1. Gently pull down on the sides of the fabric to stretch it tightly.

❷ Choose one of the permanent markers (labeled with a P). Near the center of the cloth, place five or six dots to create a circle about the size of a quarter as shown in Figure 2.

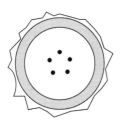

Figure 2

❸ Choose a water-soluble marker (labeled with a W) of a different color and make dots in between the permanent-marker dots in your circle. Make a note of which dots were made by each pen.

❹ Fill the dropper about half-full with water and slowly squeeze a few drops of water into the center of the circle of marker dots. Observe as the water spreads out through the fabric. Add additional drops of water if you wish, holding the dropper over the same spot. Describe what, if anything, happened to the colored dots. Do they all behave the same way?

❺ Remove the cloth and hang it on a drying line or place it on a paper towel to dry. Does the cloth look any different when dry?

Part 2: Alcohol Test

❶ Using a new piece of white fabric, repeat Part 1, steps 1–3.

 Isopropyl alcohol is intended for external use only; avoid ingestion or contact with eyes. Do not do this activity near an open flame.

❷ Half-fill the dropper with isopropyl alcohol and slowly add drops to the center of the cloth. Have students describe what happens. Do all of the dots behave the same way?

❸ Remove the cloth and hang it on a drying line or place it on a paper towel to dry. Does the cloth look any different when dry?

Teacher Notes for the Assessment

Materials

For Setup only
- scissors
- masking tape and pen for labels

Per class
- drying line or paper towels

Per group
- 2 pieces of white cloth approximately 7 inches x 7 inches
- coffee can or butter tub with plastic lid
- permanent marker
- water-soluble marker
- dropper
- 2 ounces water
- 2 ounces isopropyl alcohol (91% or greater)
- 2 disposable plastic cups, 5-ounce size or smaller

Setup

- Cut a hole out of the plastic lid of each coffee can or butter tub so that approximately ½ inch of the lid remains around the rim of the can. (See figure at left.)

- For each group, label one disposable plastic cup "water" and the other "isopropyl alcohol." Put about ¼ inch of the appropriate liquid in each.

- Label each permanent marker with a "P" and each water-soluble marker with a "W" to help prevent confusion, as some brands of markers (especially water-soluble ones) are not clearly labeled as permanent or water-soluble.

- The 7-inch x 7-inch pieces of white cloth are large enough to fit over the mouth of a typical 2-pound, 7-ounce coffee can or 2-pound butter tub with cloth to spare. If you are using larger coffee cans or butter tubs, you will need to use larger pieces of cloth. If you are using smaller cans or tubs, you may want to cut the pieces to fit the mouth with about an inch of cloth to spare.

Classroom Science from [A] to [Z]

Challenge

Review with students the idea that the Paint with Water pictures work because water dissolves the ink, allowing it to be spread around with a paintbrush. Tell students that they will now investigate a more complex process called chromatography. Explain that in chromatography, the inks dissolve and then may separate into different colors as they spread.

Tell students that their challenge is to make designs and then figure out which part of the design results from simple dissolving and which part results from color separation of the inks. Give students the Student Assessment handout (master provided) and have student groups work along with you as you demonstrate the procedure described in the handout.

Suggestions for Follow-Up

Have students compare the results of using water with those of using isopropyl alcohol. (When the cloth is treated with water, the water-soluble ink will spread out across the cloth along with the water. The permanent ink will not move. When the cloth is treated with isopropyl alcohol, the ink from the permanent marker also spreads out along with the isopropyl alcohol.)

Can students see parts of the designs that seem to result from simple dissolving? Can they see parts that result from color separation of the inks? (The ink from the water-soluble markers usually separates into the colors which were combined to make it. Scientists call this process of separation "chromatography." The permanent-marker ink is much less likely to do this.)

Have students write one important fact or idea they learned during this lesson in their science journals.

Reference

"Chromatography T-shirt Designs"; *Fun with Chemistry: A Guidebook of K–12 Activities;* Sarquis, M., Sarquis, J., Eds.; Institute for Chemical Education: Madison, WI, 1993; Vol. 2, pp 29–35.

Science Explanation

This section explains the science concepts in this lesson as well as in the "Quaint Paint" Family Science Challenge in Science Night Family Fun from A to Z. *It is intended for the teacher's information and may be modified as necessary for discussion with students.*

In the Family Science Challenge, Paint with Water pictures are used to experiment with different solvents. The colored inks on the page of a Paint with Water book are water-soluble. These water-soluble colors are applied as small dots inside the dark lines outlining the picture. The dark lines are made from water-insoluble inks. When water is applied with a paintbrush, the water dissolves some of the paint dots and the brush spreads the color across the page.

Besides testing the effect of water on these water-soluble inks, the Family Science Challenge tests the effects of other liquids. Not surprisingly, liquids that contain large amounts of water (such as vinegar) give similar results to the water. In contrast, oil has very little effect on water-soluble inks. As a rule of thumb, one substance will dissolve in another if the two substances are similar—hence the expression, "Like dissolves like." As a result, the students can conclude that the water-soluble inks do not dissolve in oil because they are not similar to oil.

Chemists often describe the nature of solvents in terms of their being "polar" or "nonpolar." Water (a polar substance) dissolves other polar materials, such as acetic acid (found in vinegar) and sugar, as well as ionic substances such as salts. Oil, on the other hand, is nonpolar. Oil dissolves other nonpolar substances such as some inks, grease, and some types of dirt; it does not dissolve salt or sugar. Isopropyl alcohol is less polar than water but more polar than oil. It will best dissolve substances that are moderately polar.

In the classroom Science Activity, students again investigate the ability of different solvents to dissolve inks. This time, one of the inks is water-soluble (and thus dissolves in both water and the isopropyl alcohol, which contains water) and the other is permanent (non-water-soluble) and thus does not dissolve in plain water but does dissolve in the isopropyl alcohol.

The Assessment uses a separation technique called radial chromatography to create a decorative pattern. Chromatography is a process in which the solvent spreads out in a radial pattern, dissolving the inks and carrying the different ink pigments along to varying degrees. Students try two solvents—water and isopropyl alcohol—because the markers used have inks that are soluble in different solvents. Again, the students see that water and isopropyl alcohol dissolve and carry water-soluble ink, and isopropyl alcohol dissolves and carries permanent ink.

In the Family Science Challenge, family teams should have noted another interesting phenomenon about the way oil affects the nature of the paper itself and causes it to appear almost transparent. (The effect is similar to that observed when paper is coated with wax to make wax paper.) This phenomenon is not very well understood. Some sources suggest that reflection of light from white paper is due in part to light scattering from the unbonded surfaces of the fibers in the paper. The various liquids poured on the paper somehow change this unbonded nature, so that the light is scattered less. Thus, reflectance decreases, allowing the light to penetrate. Other sources suggest that because paper is made of many layers of tiny fibers with air in between, the speed of light constantly changes as it passes through the material. When oil (or another similar liquid) is added, the molecules of liquid move into the spaces between the fibers. The light passes through oil and paper at about the same speed, and as a result less light is scattered and the paper appears more transparent. Most papers contain sizing materials that reduce the ability of water to wet the sheet. As a result, water does the poorest job of making the paper transparent. The sizing materials seem to have little effect on oils and certain other organic liquids.

Cross-Curricular Integration

Art and Music

- Have students experiment with watercolor pencils, such as those made by Crayola®. You can draw with these pencils as you would with typical colored pencils. Then you can paint over your drawings with water for a watercolor painting effect.
- Investigate watercolor painting.
- Study the Impressionist painters who used dot techniques (called pointillism) to create paintings. One famous example is Seurat's *Sunday Afternoon on the Island of La Grande Jatte.* The painting actually consists of thousands of tiny dots, but when you look at it from a distance the dots blend together to create the picture.
- Visit a local art museum and look at the watercolor paintings.

Mathematics

- Make chromatographs of different water-soluble black markers by placing a dot of marker on a strip of coffee filter about ½ inch from the bottom of the strip. Have students hold the strip in a cup that has about ¼ inch of water in it. The water will move up the filter strip and dissolve and separate the marker pigments. Have students measure how far each different color travels away from the original dot and record these distances on a graph.
- Have students record the different colors they observe in each chromatograph made in the above extension. Have them record the number of times each color appears in each different chromatograph. Older students can calculate the percentage of markers that use each pigment to make black. For example, if blue appears in six of 15 chromatographs, 40% of the markers use blue pigments to make black. Challenge students to use these results to guess what colors a new brand of water-soluble black marker is made of, then prepare a chromatograph to verify their guesses.

Social Studies

- Investigate how dyes, markers, and paints were invented and who invented them.

Just for Fun

- Have each student use chromatography to make a quilt square and then sign it with a permanent marker. Sew the squares together to make a quilted wall hanging and donate it to a nursing home or raffle it off and donate the money to a children's shelter.

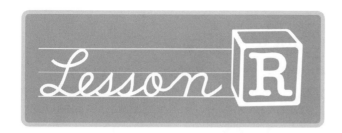

Reactive Colors

*Enrich the "**Radical Writing**" activity in the book* Science Night Family Fun from A to Z *or use as a stand-alone lesson on color change indicators.*

Students classify household products as acidic, basic, or neutral and investigate grape-juice concentrate as an acid-base indicator.

Key Science Topics

- acid-base indicators
- acids and bases
- chemical reactions
- household chemistry

Time Required

Science Activity 1

Setup	10–15	minutes
Performance	10–20	minutes
Cleanup	5	minutes

Science Activity 2

Setup	15–20	minutes plus drying time
Performance	10–15	minutes
Cleanup	5	minutes

 Overview

······························ # National Science Education Standards

Science as Inquiry Standards

- Abilities Necessary to Do Scientific Inquiry
  Students conduct simple experiments to determine what happens when goldenrod and grape-juice papers are exposed to acids and bases.

  Students plan and conduct investigations to determine whether color-change markers use acid-base reactions.

  Students use their observations of goldenrod paper to determine the acid-base natures of familiar household solutions.

  Students use their observations to draw conclusions regarding the colors of goldenrod and grape-juice paper under acidic and basic conditions.

  Students evaluate and analyze their own observations and investigations and those of their classmates.

  Students discuss their observations and conclusions with their adult partners and with their classmates.

Physical Science

- Properties of Objects and Materials
  Materials such as vinegar, baking soda in water, and various household solutions have the property of being acidic, basic, or neutral.

- Properties and Changes of Properties in Matter
  The color of goldenrod and grape-juice papers changes when the acidity of the environment changes.

History and Nature of Science

- Science as a Human Endeavor
  Students learn how people have developed and used inks and dyes in espionage.

Science Activity 1

Materials

2–3 strips of yellow goldenrod paper • 2 strips of "red" goldenrod paper • cotton-tipped swab halves • baking soda solution • water • vinegar • dishwashing liquid • small cups • masking tape and pen for labels • pencil • spoon • several household products • water to make solutions

Challenge

Can you use goldenrod paper to determine the acidic, basic, or neutral nature of household products?

Procedure

❶ If you did the "Radical Writing" Family Science Challenge, recall the color the yellow goldenrod paper turned when the four solutions listed below were painted on it:
  • baking soda solution (a basic solution),
  • water (a neutral liquid),
  • vinegar (an acidic solution), and
  • dishwashing liquid (a basic solution).

Record the colors in Observation Table 1 (next page). If you did not do the "Radical Writing" activity or if you are unsure of the answers, follow steps 2–5 to test the four solutions.

Figure 1

❷ Fold a strip of goldenrod paper into four equal sections as shown in Figure 1. Then unfold the strip to reveal the four sections.

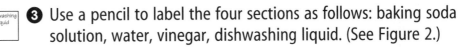

Figure 2

❸ Use a pencil to label the four sections as follows: baking soda solution, water, vinegar, dishwashing liquid. (See Figure 2.)

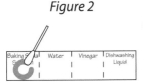

Figure 3

❹ Dip a clean cotton-tipped swab in the baking soda solution, and rub it onto the "Baking Soda Solution" section of the goldenrod paper. Record your observations in Observation Table 1.

❺ Repeat step 4 with the other three liquids, using a clean swab for each test liquid. Be sure to rub each liquid on its labeled area of the goldenrod paper. Record your observations.

Observation Table 1				
Test solution	Nature of test solution	Color of *yellow* goldenrod paper after application of test liquid (steps ❹ and ❺)	Color of *red* goldenrod paper after application of test liquid (step ❻)	
			Predicted	Observed
vinegar	acid			
baking soda solution	base			
water	neutral			
dishwashing liquid	base			

❻ Use what you learned about the color change goldenrod paper undergoes to predict what color the *red* goldenrod paper will turn when each of the liquids listed in Observation Table 1 is rubbed on it. (Red goldenrod paper has been treated with baking soda solution.) Record your predictions. Now follow steps 2–5 to test the four liquids on the *red* goldenrod paper. Record your observations.

❼ List the household products you will be testing in the "Household Test Solution" column of Observation Table 2 below. In the "Prediction" column, predict whether these solutions are acids, bases, or neutral.

Observation Table 2				
Household test solution	Prediction: Is it an acid, base, or neutral? (step ❼)	Color of goldenrod paper after the test solution is added (step ❾)		Conclusion: Is it an acid, base, or neutral? (step ❿)
		to the *yellow* paper	to the *red* paper	

8 Prepare a small amount of each test solution in a cup. If you are testing liquid household products, you can use them as they are. If you are testing solids, you must first dissolve them in water. If any solids are in tablet form, they should be crushed first. To dissolve a small amount of a solid (about the size of a pea), add just enough water to cover the solid and stir. Don't worry about any undissolved residue that might remain at the bottom of the cup. Label each cup.

9 Use both a yellow strip and a red strip of goldenrod paper to test the solutions you made or collected following the method described in steps 2–5. (Depending on the number of solutions you are testing, you may need to fold your paper to make more than four sections.) Record your observations.

10 Use what you know about goldenrod colors and your observations to conclude whether each household solution is an acid, base, or neutral. Record your conclusions in Observation Table 2.

Names _____   _____

_____   _____

Science Activity 2

Materials

baking soda • water • vinegar • plastic cup • spoon • piece of grape-juice indicator paper • pencil • cotton-tipped swabs • grape-juice concentrate • 3 test tubes • masking tape and pen for labels

Challenge

Determine how grape juice works as an acid-base indicator.

Procedure

Figure 1

1 Make a baking soda solution by dissolving 1 spoonful baking soda in 3 spoonsful water in a cup. Stir to mix. Don't worry if some of the baking soda remains undissolved.

2 Record the color of the grape-juice indicator paper at the top of Observation Table 1. Fold the strip into three equal sections as shown in Figure 1. Unfold the strip to reveal the three sections.

Baking Soda Solution	Water	Vinegar

Figure 2

3 Use a pencil to label the three sections as follows: Baking Soda Solution, Water, and Vinegar. (See Figure 2.)

4 Dip a clean cotton-tipped swab in the baking soda solution and rub it onto the "Baking Soda Solution" section of the grape-juice indicator paper. Record your observations in Observation Table 1.

5 Repeat step 4 with the other two liquids, using a clean swab for each test solution. Be sure to rub each test solution on its labeled area of the paper. Record your observations.

Observation Table 1			
Original color of grape-juice paper: _____			
Test solution applied	Color of grape juice paper (steps **4** and **5**)	Test solution applied	Color of paper (step **6**)
baking soda		vinegar applied to baking soda spot	
water			
vinegar		baking soda solution applied to vinegar spot	

? *Use what you previously learned about the acid-base nature of these test liquids to summarize the behavior of grape juice as an acid-base indicator.*

_____

_____

_____

_____

6 Determine whether the color changes are reversible by rubbing vinegar on top of the baking soda spot on the grape-juice indicator paper and rubbing baking soda solution over the vinegar spot. Record your observations in Observation Table 1.

7 Label three test tubes as shown in Figure 3 and add about ½ inch of grape-juice concentrate to each tube.

8 Add about ½ inch of the appropriate test liquid to its labeled test tube, put your thumb over the mouth of the test tube, and shake to mix. Continue adding small amounts of each liquid to its test tube until you see a color change in at least one test tube or until the test tube is half full. Record your observations in Observation Table 2.

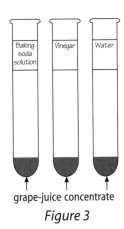

grape-juice concentrate

Figure 3

Observation Table 2	
Contents of test tube	Color of solution (step **8**)
Grape-juice concentrate and baking soda solution	
Grape-juice concentrate and vinegar	
Grape-juice concentrate and water	

Teacher Notes for Science Activity 1

Materials

Per class
- 2-L plastic bottle of baking soda solution (See Setup for preparation.)

Per group
- 2–3, 1-inch x 8½-inch strips of goldenrod paper

Not all brands of goldenrod paper contain the indicator dye that is required for this activity. Brands of goldenrod paper that have worked for this activity include Astro Bright's "Galaxy Gold" paper (style #100126) and Mead paper. However, even if using the papers mentioned here, test them before using. (See Setup.) Goldenrod paper for this activity is available from Terrific Science Books, Kits, & More, 513/727-3269, #GRP01.

- 2, 1-inch x 8½-inch strips of "red" goldenrod paper (See Setup for preparation)
- (optional) test solutions for review of Family Science Challenge results:
  - water
  - baking soda solution
  - vinegar
  - dishwashing liquid
- household products to test for acidity or basicity, such as the following (provide about 1 teaspoon of each or 1 tablet):
  - salt
  - sugar
  - aspirin
  - antacid tablets
  - shampoo
  - detergent
  - milk of magnesia
  - colorless soft drinks
  - colorless or pale juices
  - milk
- 8–10 cotton-tipped swab halves (See Setup for preparation.)
- 5 or more cups

Provide a cup and a swab for each solution tested, including test solutions for review of Family Science Challenge results if students are doing that step.

- small cup of water (for making test solutions from household products)
- spoon
- masking tape and pen for labels

Safety

If you choose to use solutions other than those listed in the Materials list, test them ahead of time. Some household items should NOT be included because of their reactivity, corrosiveness, flammability, or toxicity. DO NOT USE the following liquids:
- drain cleaners or other household bases that react with cleaners containing ammonia to generate ammonia gas;

- hypochlorite ("chlorine") bleach (for example, Clorox®), which reacts with acids found in vinegar, soft drinks, citrus drinks, and some cleaners to produce highly toxic chlorine gas;
- antifreeze that contains ethylene glycol. Ethylene glycol is very toxic, and ingestion of even a small amount can be fatal.

Setup

- Always test the goldenrod paper (even if you have used a particular brand before) to be sure it contains acid-base indicators in the dye. Since goldenrod paper is dyed in different ways, even paper from the same supplier may not always be the same. A quick method for testing paper is to spray it with Windex® with Ammonia-D to see if a color change occurs. (The paper should turn dark orange or red.) Caution: Do not get ammonia in your eyes—it will cause severe damage. Should contact occur, immediately wash the eyes with large quantities of cool water for at least 15 minutes.

- Cut the goldenrod paper into approximately 1-inch x 8½-inch strips. Each 8½-inch x 11-inch sheet of paper will yield 11 pieces of this size. Each group will use four strips, two untreated and two treated to become "red" goldenrod paper. (See below.) If groups do the optional steps 2–5, they will need an additional strip of untreated paper.

- Cut the cotton-tipped swabs in half.

- Prepare the baking soda solution in an empty 1- or 2-L plastic bottle by almost filling the bottle with water and adding 13 tablespoons baking soda for each liter of water used. Cap the bottle and shake well to mix. Some undissolved baking soda will probably remain at the bottom of the bottle; this is normal. Label the bottle. This baking soda solution can be used by students as a test solution and to make the "red" goldenrod paper.

- Prepare the "red" goldenrod paper as follows: Pour some baking soda solution into a shallow dish. Dip 1-inch x 8½-inch goldenrod paper strips into the solution. They will turn red. Lay the strips to dry on a piece of plastic or waxed paper.

Answers and Observations

Observation Table 1				
Test solution	Nature of test solution	Color of *yellow* goldenrod paper after application of test solution (steps ❹ and ❺)	Color of *red* goldenrod paper after application of test solution (step ❻)	
			Predicted	Observed
vinegar	acid	yellow		yellow
baking soda solution	base	red		red
water	neutral	yellow		red
dishwashing liquid	base	red		red

Observation Table 2				
Household test solution	Prediction: Is it an acid, base, or neutral? (step ❼)	Color of goldenrod paper after the test solution is added (step ❾)		Conclusion: Is it an acid, base, or neutral? (step ❿)
		to the *yellow* paper	to the *red* paper	
table salt		yellow	red	neutral
sugar		yellow	red	neutral
aspirin tablets		yellow	yellow	acid
antacid tablets		red	red	base
shampoo		red	red	base
detergent		red	red	base
colorless soft drink		yellow	yellow	acid
milk		yellow	yellow	acid
colorless or pale juice		yellow	yellow	acid

Suggestions for Follow-Up

Have students describe how they used the goldenrod paper to determine the acidic or basic nature of the household products, and then have them share their results with the class and discuss similarities or differences.

Teacher Notes for Science Activity 2

Materials

For Setup only

- purple grape-juice concentrate (thawed)
- porous white paper such as construction paper, blotter paper, white paper towels, or coffee filters

You will need enough to give each student one 1-inch x 8½-inch strip.

- scissors
- flat dish or baking pan
- plastic wrap or waxed paper

Per group
- 3 test solutions:
  - 1 teaspoon water
  - 1 teaspoon baking soda plus 3 teaspoons water
  - 1 teaspoon vinegar
- small (about 8-ounce) plastic disposable cup
- plastic spoon
- 1-inch x 8½-inch strip of grape-juice indicator paper (See Setup for preparation)
- pencil
- 3 cotton-tipped swabs
- grape-juice concentrate
- 3 test tubes
- masking tape and pen for labels

Safety

Do not allow students to drink the grape juice used in this activity.

Setup

To make the grape-juice indicator paper you will need purple grape-juice concentrate (thawed) and porous white paper such as construction paper, blotter paper, white paper towels, or coffee filters. Cut the paper into 1-inch x 8½-inch strips. Pour the grape-juice concentrate into a flat dish or baking pan. Soak the paper in the grape-juice solution. Lay the purple paper strips on plastic or waxed paper to dry overnight. To dry the strips more quickly, or if the weather is very humid, lay the wet strips on a cookie sheet and dry them in an oven at 150–200° F for several hours. DO NOT heat above 200°, because the grape juice could char.

Answers and Observations

Observation Table 1			
Original color of grape-juice paper: ___purple___			
Test solution applied	Color of grape juice paper (steps ❹ and ❺)	Test solution applied	Color of paper (step ❻)
baking soda	The paper turns green.	vinegar applied to baking soda spot	The paper turns purple or reddish-purple.
water	The paper stays the same color.		
vinegar	The paper stays the same color.	baking soda solution applied to vinegar spot	The paper turns green.

❺ *Use what you previously learned about the acid-base nature of these test liquids to summarize the behavior of grape juice as an acid-base indicator.*

Since grape juice is acidic, the grape-juice paper is normally the acid color. It changes color when it comes in contact with a base, but it stays the same color when it comes in contact with another acid or a neutral substance.

Observation Table 2	
Contents of test tube	Color of solution (step ❽)
Grape-juice concentrate and baking soda solution	green
Grape-juice concentrate and vinegar	reddish purple
Grape-juice concentrate and water	reddish-purple, although it may get lighter

Suggestions for Follow-Up

As a class, discuss how the grape-juice indicator paper is similar to goldenrod paper. Have the class test other common substances to see whether they are acid-base indicators. Common indicators include Red Zinger tea and the juice from blueberries, cherries, and red cabbage. The class may also try other substances such as coffee, tea, and assorted fruit juices.

Assessment

Materials

Per group
- white paper
- set of color-change markers, including colored markers and developer pen
  Color-change markers write in one color and then reveal another color when a special developer pen is used to write over the color. One popular brand is Crayola® Changeables markers. Not all of the markers in a set will change color when the test acids and bases are applied. Test the markers you plan to use in advance to make sure that some of them show a change.

- assorted acid or base test solutions from Activities 1 and 2
  Depending on which activities students have done, provide test solutions that they have already determined to be either acids or bases.

Challenge

Give students a chance to explore the color-change effects of the markers. Then challenge students to develop a procedure using the materials you have made available to test whether any of the markers in the set change color because they contain an acid-base indicator, similar to goldenrod paper or grape juice. Have students outline their plans, conduct the tests, and record the data. Students should then share their results with the class and discuss the following questions:

- Experimental design:
  - What substances did you use to test the idea that the pens contain acid-base indicators?
  - Why did you choose these substances?
  - How did you know which substances were acids and which were bases?
  - How did you keep track of your results?

- Results:
  - Were any ink colors affected by acids?
  - Were any ink colors not affected by acids?
  - Did different kinds of acids give the same result?
  - Were any ink colors affected by bases?
  - Were any ink colors not affected by bases?
  - Did different kinds of bases give the same result?
  - Which ink colors definitely contain acid-base indicators? How do you know?
  - Can you be certain that any of the marker colors do not contain acid-base indicators? Why or why not?

After completing the class discussion, have students write one important fact or idea they learned in this lesson in their science journals.

 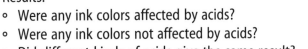

 **Assessment**

Sample Results

Below are some sample results with Crayola® Changeables markers tested with baking soda solution and vinegar. Note that some inks may not change color in the student experiments, or they may change to different colors than you would get by using the special developer pen provided with the set. These discrepancies are not due to student error. They occur because the marker ink contains other dyes in addition to acid-base indicators. Some other dyes are not affected by an acid or a base but can change colors reversibly due to a totally different type of chemical reaction called oxidation-reduction, or redox. (Bleaching and indigo dyeing are common examples of redox systems.)

Results when using Crayola® Changeables™ color change markers*			
Original color of ink on paper	Color after applying developer pen	Color after applying vinegar	Color after applying baking soda
red	goldenrod	red	no change
orange	yellow	orange	no change
green	purple	green	purple
blue	aqua	blue	no change
orchid	marigold	orchid	marigold
purple	coral	purple	no change
* Color names are Crayola brand names.			

Science Explanation

This section explains the science concepts in this lesson as well as in the "Radical Writing" Family Science Challenge in Science Night Family Fun from A to Z. *It is intended for the teacher's information and may be modified as necessary for discussion with students.*

Goldenrod paper is a common color of office copy paper. Some brands of goldenrod paper are dyed with a chemical that is an acid-base indicator. An acid-base indicator is a dye that exhibits different colors in acidic and basic solutions. Goldenrod paper is golden yellow in acidic and red in basic environments. Because most paper is itself acidic, we typically see the yellow acidic form of the dye when goldenrod paper is purchased.

When yellow goldenrod paper is treated with vinegar (an acid), no color change is observed, because the yellow dye is already in an acidic environment. However, when the yellow paper is treated with the baking soda solution (a base), the area turns orange to red, the basic color of the dye. When the paper dries, its red color intensifies. This "baking soda treated" goldenrod paper turns yellow when exposed to an acid and remains red when exposed to a base. When either color of paper is wetted with water, a neutral liquid (neither an acid nor a base), no color change occurs.

As seen in the Family Science Challenge and classroom Science Activity 1, goldenrod paper strips can be used to indicate whether aqueous solutions of common household chemicals are acidic, basic, or neutral. The chart below summarizes results of such a test with different liquids.

When the yellow goldenrod paper treated with a test solution...	and the red paper treated with the solution...	then the solution is...	Examples include (aqueous solutions of)
stays yellow	turns yellow	acidic	vinegar, soft drinks, lemon juice .
turns red	stays red	basic	baking soda, detergents, soaps, antacids
stays yellow	stays red	neutral	water, table salt, sugar

In classroom Science Activity 2, students learned that grape juice also contains an acid-base indicator. It works very similarly to the goldenrod except that the colors are different, as shown below.

When the purple paper treated with a test solution...	and the green paper treated with the solution...	then the solution is...	Examples include (aqueous solutions of)
stays purple	turns purple	acidic	vinegar, soft drinks, lemon juice
turns green	stays green	basic	baking soda, detergents, soaps, antacids
stays purple	stays green	neutral	water, table salt, sugar

As seen in the Assessment, some brands of color-change markers use acid-base reactions to produce the color changes they are known for. These markers use two special ink formulas—one for the colored markers in the set and one for the colorless "developer" pens—to create the effect.

Both the markers and developer pens contain a solvent (usually water), a glycol or other humectant (to keep the pens from drying out), and a nonsudsing detergent or other wetting agent (to increase the rate at which the ink spreads across the paper). In addition to these ingredients, the colored markers typically contain two different dyes and an acid such as citric acid. The developer pens typically contain both a base and a redox agent such as sodium sulfite (Na_2SO_3).

Under acidic conditions, such as when a colored marker is applied to paper, the "acid color" is visible. When the developer pen is used, the color changes. This color change can be the result of one or a combination of factors, including the following:
- The base in the developing pen causes the dye on the paper to change color.
- The redox agent causes the dye to change color.
- One of the dyes in the color marker is affected by the base and/or the redox agent while the second dye is not. For example, the developer pen's ink can render one dye colorless, allowing the second dye, which is unaffected, to become visible.

In the student experiments, some of the markers may not change color in the presence of the test acids or bases. These inks may actually be sensitive to acids and bases but require different concentrations of acids or bases than in the test substances. Additionally, some of the inks may also require a redox agent (as contained in the developer pen) to change color.

Reference

Anderson, C.; Katz, D. "A Mark of Color" Lab Activity, *ChemMatters,* Oct 1998. http://chemcenter.acs.org/ncw/activ.html (downloadable PDF file of article, accessed July 1999).

Cross-Curricular Integration

Art and Music

- Use goldenrod or grape-juice paper and vinegar and baking soda solutions to create a design or picture. Share the picture with family or friends and explain how it was made.

Language Arts

- As a class, write to the company that made the goldenrod paper used in the investigations. Describe how the paper was used and ask for information about the goldenrod dye.
- Read *Nate the Great,* by Marjorie Weinman Sharmat (Young Yearling, ISBN 044046126X).
  With three-color illustrations, neighborhood detective Nate investigates the disappearance of his friend Annie's favorite painting.

Social Studies

- Investigate how secret messages involving color change inks or other chemical reactions have been used in espionage throughout history—even as long ago as the American Revolution.

Sound Off

Enrich the **"Singing Straws"** *activity in the book* Science Night Family Fun from A to Z *or use as a stand-alone lesson on sound.*

Students explore Singing Straws with holes in them.

.... **Key Science Topics**

- pitch
- sound
- vibrations

.... **Average Time Required**

Setup	5–10	minutes
Performance	10–15	minutes
Cleanup	5	minutes

. . . . **National Science Education Standards**

Science as Inquiry Standards

- Abilities Necessary to Do Scientific Inquiry

  Students make a Singing Straw with a reed and use it to investigate the relationship between the length of the straw and the pitch of the sound.

  Students use their observations to determine that Singing Straws with shorter air columns have higher pitches.

  Students further investigate the effect of changing the length of the air column on the sound by using straws with holes that can be covered or uncovered.

  Students conduct an investigation to determine how the amount of water in a bottle affects the pitch of the sound.

Physical Science

- Position and Motion of Objects

  Sound is produced by a vibrating column of air

  Shorter vibrating columns of air have higher pitches than do longer vibrating columns.

History and Nature of Science

- Science as a Human Endeavor

  Students learn that when people design musical instruments they are applying physics principles. People have been doing this for centuries.

Science Activity

Materials

drinking straws with holes in them • scissors • tape

Challenge

What changes result when holes are added to the singing straw?

Procedure

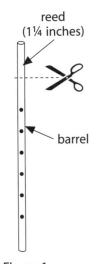

reed
(1¼ inches)

barrel

Figure 1

❶ Cut across the fat straw at a point 1¼ inches from one end. The longer straw piece will be the barrel of the singing straw, and the shorter piece will be the reed. (See Figure 1.)

❷ To prepare the reed, flatten the top of the shorter piece and cut the top into a wedged point. Then cut two short slits at the bottom blunt end. (See Figure 2.)

❸ Slip the square end of the reed over the long straw piece (barrel) as shown in Figure 3. Slide the end of the barrel up into the reed until it is above the bottom slits of the reed but below the top slits. Once the reed is in position, tape it to the barrel as shown in Figure 4.

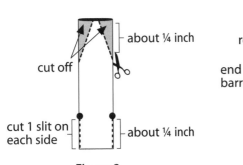

about ¼ inch

cut off

cut 1 slit on
each side

about ¼ inch

Figure 2

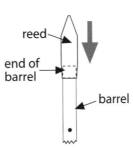

reed

end of
barrel

barrel

Figure 3

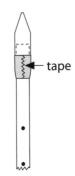

tape

Figure 4

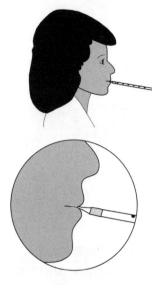

Figure 5

❹ Press the reed and top of the barrel together with your lips and blow through the reed as shown in Figure 5. (Remember to blow through only your own straw—no one else's.) Adjust the pressure of your lips until you achieve sound. It will probably sound like a kazoo. It may help to moisten the reed and flatten it between your teeth to make a better seal between your lips and the reed.

? *What did you observe?*

_____

_____

_____

❺ Try covering and uncovering different combinations of the finger holes while you blow.

? *What did you observe?*

_____

_____

_____

Teacher Notes for the Science Activity

Materials

For Setup only
- one-hole punch

Per group
- scissors
- tape

Per student
- drinking straw

You may want to provide extras in case students are unsuccessful at first.

Setup

Flatten each straw and use the hole punch to carefully punch six small, shallow holes on one side down the length of the straws. (See figure below.) Place the holes close enough together to allow easy finger positioning. Be careful not to punch the holes too deep, or small fingers will have trouble sealing them.

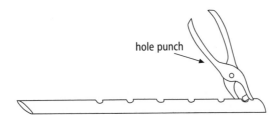

hole punch

Suggestion for Follow-Up

As a class, discuss what happened to the sound when the students covered or uncovered different combinations of holes as they blew through the straws. How do they think covering and uncovering the holes changes the sounds?

Assessment

Materials

Per group
- 3 glass bottles with narrow mouths
  Soft-drink bottles work well. All of the bottles need to be the same size and shape.

- water
- (optional) food color

Per student
- drinking straw

Resources

Eight-ounce or 20-ounce glass soft-drink bottles are ideal for this activity, as they are sold in packs of six or eight and are the same size and shape.

Setup

- For each group, leave one bottle empty, fill one about one-third full of water, and fill the last one about two-thirds full of water. To make the water more visible, add a few drops of food color. Arrange the bottles so they are not in order of water volume.

Challenge

Show students the three bottles containing different amounts of colored water. Ask students if they have ever "played" a glass bottle by blowing across the mouth of the bottle. Use a straw to demonstrate with one bottle. Challenge students to use what they have learned about sound to arrange the three bottles in order from the one producing the lowest-pitched sound to the one producing the highest-pitched sound and to explain why the different bottles produce different pitches. Tell students to use only their own straws when playing the bottles.

Have students write one important fact or idea they learned during this lesson in their science journals.

Science Explanation

This section explains the science concepts in this lesson as well as in the "Singing Straws" Family Science Challenge in Science Night Family Fun from A to Z. *It is intended for the teacher's information and may be modified as necessary for discussion with students.*

The sound of the Singing Straw is caused by the vibration of a reed and the column of air that passes through the straw. The students can feel these vibrations from the moving air on their tongues, lips, and fingers when they use the Singing Straw. The longer the column of vibrating air, the longer the wavelength of sound and the lower the frequency (pitch). The shorter the column, the shorter the wavelength of the sound and the higher the frequency (pitch). Cutting the straw while it is being played makes the sound higher because it shortens the column of vibrating air. Sliding the thin straw in and out of the Singing Straw shortens and lengthens the air column and changes the sound accordingly.

The length of the air column is also the key to the variations in the sounds in the classroom Science Activity. If holes near the reed are uncovered, the air column is short and the pitch is high. If the holes near the reed are covered, the air column is longer and the pitch is lower. Similarly, the lower the water levels in the bottles in the Assessment, the longer the air column and the lower the pitch. Nearly full bottles have shorter air columns and correspondingly higher pitches. The action of the turbulent air flowing over the tops of the bottles causes the vibrations, which subsequently cause the bottles and the air inside to vibrate.

A difference in the length of the air column is why piccolos produce a higher-frequency sound than flutes, and why trombones produce a lower sound than trumpets. The length and diameter of the vibrating air column are related to the length of the instrument and its characteristic pitch.

Cross-Curricular Integration

Art and Music

- Compare the sizes of different woodwind instruments. How does the size of an instrument affect the pitch of the sound it makes? After seeing the instruments, can students hear an instrument and guess its size without seeing it?
- Investigate and listen to different types of woodwind instruments from different countries. How are they similar and how are they different?
- Investigate how different musical instruments produce vibrations and change the pitch of sounds. In particular, investigate how vibrations are produced in wind instruments such as flutes and brass instruments (such as trumpets, french horns, and trombones), which don't use reeds.

Language Arts

- Write a short story to be read out loud using different pitches for different characters in the story.
- Read aloud or have students read the following book:
  - *Goggles,* by Ezra Jack Keats (Viking, ISBN 0-698-71157-3)
    In this classic story about Peter and his neighborhood friends, Peter and his friend Archie find motorcycle goggles, and bigger boys try to take them away. As part of their plan to foil the bigger boys, Peter and Archie direct sound through a pipe.

Life Science

- Research how different living creatures make sounds. In every case, something is vibrating. What is vibrating when a cricket "chirps?" What about when a horse neighs?
- Read more about how human vocal cords work and how ears "hear" sounds.

Mathematics

- Research how the frequency of vibrations in a musical scale are related mathematically. Find out the relationships between the notes that make up a major chord, minor chord, or even more complicated chords like 7ths and diminished.

Social Studies

- Trace the history of reed instruments, such as the oboe, clarinet, or bagpipes. Learn about the difference between single-reed and double-reed instruments.

Just for Fun

- Invite a reed instrument player to your class to explain his/her instrument and demonstrate its sounds.

Tilt-a-Whirl Water

Enrich the **"Tornado in a Bottle"** *activity in the book* Science Night Family Fun from A to Z *or use as a stand-alone lesson on circular motion.*

Students investigate how salt and/or detergent makes a water vortex more or less visible.

.... **Key Science Topics**

- circular motion
- soap bubbles
- vortex

.... **Average Time Required**

Setup	10–15	minutes
Performance	10	minutes
Cleanup	5	minutes

············· # National Science Education Standards

Science as Inquiry Standards

- Abilities Necessary to Do Scientific Inquiry
  Students investigate what effect swirling a bottle has on how long it takes to empty the bottle of water during the Family Science Challenge.

  Students plan and conduct an investigation to see how the size and shape of a bottle affect the vortex produced.

  Students use their observations to develop cause-and-effect relationships about what impacts the additives and the size and shape of the container have on the vortices produced.

  Students investigate the visual impact of adding soap and/or salt to the "tornadoes."

  Students analyze their own observations and explanations and those of their classmates during class discussions.

  Students discuss their observations and the results of their investigations with their adult partners and with their classmates.

Physical Science

- Position and Motion of Objects
  Swirling the water in a bottle causes it to form a vortex—a tornado or whirlpool shape—with water on the outside and air on the inside of the vortex.

- Motions and Forces
  Gravity and the circular motion created by the person swirling the bottle cause the vortices to form and the water in the Family Science Challenge to transfer from one bottle to another.

Earth Science

- Changes in the Earth and Sky
  Students learn about the weather condition known as a tornado and where tornadoes strike.

Science Activity

Materials

1-L or smaller clear, colorless plastic bottle with cap • water
• ½ teaspoon salt • toothpick • dishwashing liquid

Challenge

How do additives affect a "Tornado in a Bottle?"

Procedure

❶ Fill the bottle about three-quarters full with water and replace the cap tightly.

❷ Swirl the bottle vigorously in a continuous circular motion. (This is often easier to do if it is sitting on a flat surface.)

❓ *What do you observe in the bottle? Draw a picture of what you see in the appropriate space in the Observation Table on the next page.*

❸ Open the bottle and add ½ teaspoon salt. Replace the cap and shake to dissolve the salt. Swirl as you did in step 2 and record your observations by drawing in the table.

❹ Open the bottle. Dab the toothpick tip in dishwashing liquid. Lightly touch the soap-coated tip to the salt-water solution.

❺ Replace the cap. Do not shake the bottle, but gently invert it a few times to mix the solution.

❻ Now swirl the bottle as you did in step 2 and draw your observations in the table.

❼ Open the bottle and dispose of the contents. Refill the bottle with water to within 1–2 inches of the top. Add dishwashing liquid as in step 4, but do not add salt.

❽ Replace the cap and invert the bottle a few times to gently mix the solution. Swirl the bottle as you did in step 2 and draw your observations in the table.

Observation Table

Water	Water and Salt
Water, Salt, and Dishwashing Liquid	**Water and Dishwashing Liquid**

Teacher Notes for the Science Activity

Materials

Per group
- 1-L or smaller clear, colorless plastic bottle with cap
- water
- ½ teaspoon salt
- toothpick
- 2–3 drops dishwashing liquid
- bucket or sink to dispose of water

Answers and Observations

? *Observation Table*
In all cases a whirlpool, vortex, or "tornado" is formed within the bottle.

Suggestions for Follow-Up

As a class, discuss which solution produced the most visible tornado-like vortex. *The water, salt, and dishwashing liquid usually produces the most visible vortex.* How were the tornadoes different? How were they similar? *The tornadoes are similar, but the ones with the additives (especially the one with both salt and dishwashing liquid) are easier to see than the one with water alone.*

Reference

"Tornado in a Bottle"; *Fun with Chemistry: A Guidebook of K–12 Activities,* 2nd ed.; Sarquis, M., Sarquis, J., Eds.; Institute for Chemical Education: Madison, WI 1991; Vol. 2, pp 319–321.

Assessment

Materials

Per student or group
- different sizes and shapes of clear, colorless jars with lids
- water, salt, and dishwashing liquid solution

Challenge

Challenge students to design an experiment to determine what effect the shape and size of the container have on the vortex that is created when the container is swirled. Have students write or discuss a plan for their experiment. Have students carry out the experiment and record their observations. Hold a class discussion on what the findings were. Have students compare the vortices in the jars with the ones they observed in the bottles.

Ask students to characterize how the size and shape of the container affect the vortices. For example, does a wider container cause a larger hole in the center of the vortex? Does a taller container cause a taller vortex? Show students a container they have not tested before and have them use their observations to predict what kind of vortex this container would produce. Discuss their predictions, then produce a vortex in the container to test their predictions and discuss the results.

After this discussion, have the students write one important fact or idea they learned in this lesson in their science journals.

Science Explanation

This section explains the science concepts in this lesson as well as in the "Tornado in a Bottle" Family Science Challenge in Science Night Family Fun from A to Z. *It is intended for the teacher's information and may be modified as necessary for discussion with students.*

In the Family Science Challenge, families create a vortex in the liquid inside the Tornado in a Bottle toy by swirling the bottle in a circular motion. The vortex is visible because of small soap bubbles that are created by the swirling.

In the classroom Science Activity, students investigate how different additives affect a Tornado in a Bottle toy. Typically when soap dissolves in water, soap bubbles form at the surface. In the motionless bottle, the surface is parallel to the Earth's surface. However, as you swirl the bottle in a circular motion, more of the solution is pushed out to the sides of the bottle, producing a vortex similar to the one we associate with a tornado. In this process, the surface of the solution actually moves from the horizontal to the cone-like vortex. Small soap bubbles at this surface make the vortex visible. The salt in the solution helps to stabilize the surface soap bubbles because it works to prevent their dispersion throughout the solution.

The Glug-Glug Bottle used in the Family Science Challenge is an example of a bottle or tube that can drain. This type of bottle illustrates two other interesting properties of vortices of this type:
- As the liquid drains through the neck, it actually moves faster.
- The vortex that forms in this process lasts much longer (typically until most of the liquid has drained out) than the one observed in the Tornado in a Bottle toy (where the liquid cannot drain out).

Families then discover that applying the same circular motion used in the Tornado in a Bottle toy to the Glug-Glug Bottle speeds up the transfer of the water from one of the connected bottles to the other. During this process a tunnel actually exists in the middle of the liquid. This tunnel lets air travel from the bottom bottle to the top bottle without having to be forced through the water. This simultaneous movement of the air and water allows the water to move more quickly from the top to the bottom bottle.

Cross-Curricular Integration

Earth Science

- Investigate how bathtubs drain. Discuss the myth that draining water spins in one direction in the northern hemisphere and the other direction in the southern hemisphere.
- Discuss what tornadoes are and how they are created.

Language Arts

- Read aloud or have students read one or more of the following books:
  - *The Storm,* by Marc Harshman (Cobblehill, ISBN 0525651500)
    A boy in a wheelchair saves the animals on his farm during a tornado. Students can respond to the book by writing about what they would do in a tornado.
  - *The Big Storm,* by Bruce Hiscock (Atheneum, ISBN 0689317700)
    In a creative retelling of the events surrounding the great storm of April 1982, Hiscock explores both United States geography and the basics of weather processes.
  - *Cloudy with a Chance of Meatballs,* by Judi Barnett (Aladdin, ISBN 0689707495)
    Life is delicious in the town of Chewandswallow where it rains soup and juice, snows mashed potatoes, and blows storms of hamburgers—until the weather takes a turn for the worse.
  - *Pickles to Pittsburgh,* by Judi Barnett (Aladdin, ISBN 0689801041)
    In this sequel to Cloudy with a Chance of Meatballs, *Kate and Henry eagerly await Grandpa's return from an unusual vacation.*
- Have students write a safety handbook on precautions to take when a tornado warning is sounded. In their handbook, they should discuss the difference between a tornado watch and a tornado warning.

Mathematics

- Have the class keep a record of newspaper accounts of tornadoes occurring in the United States for the months of March and April. The report should include where the tornado occurred and the dollar amount of damage done.
- Have the class use statistics taken from a recent weather almanac to make a graph of the number of tornadoes per year for your state and surrounding states (or for a state where tornadoes occur).

Social Studies

- Investigate what areas in the U.S. have the most tornadoes. Find these areas, including "Tornado Alley," on a map.

Just for Fun

- Show a video of tornadoes. Libraries, parents, or a video rental store may be able to provide these.
- Invite a meteorologist or storm chaser to talk about tornadoes with the class.

Useful Shapes

Enrich the **"Under Construction"** *activity in the book* Science Night Family Fun from A to Z *or use as a stand-alone lesson on engineering and geometry.*

Students explore different geometric shapes and decide which shapes would be best for use in bridge building.

Key Science Topics

- engineering
- design
- geometric shapes
- strength of materials

Average Time Required

Setup	15	minutes
Performance	30	minutes
Cleanup	5	minutes

· · · · · · · · · · · · · · # National Science Education Standards

Science as Inquiry Standards

- Abilities Necessary to Do Scientific Inquiry
  Students investigate various folded three-dimensional paper shapes and determine their relative strengths.

  Students investigate and compare the strength and design of the corrugated cardboard.

  Students discuss their results with their adult partners.

Physical Science

- Properties of Objects and Materials
  Objects have many observable properties, including size, shape, and the ability to bear a load.

Science and Technology

- Abilities of Technological Design
  Students evaluate the strengths of potential bridge components and propose the best structural design.

History and Nature of Science

- Science as a Human Endeavor
  Students discover some of the principles involved in designing and building bridges.

Science Activity

Materials

tongue depressors or craft sticks • paper fasteners or plastic ties

Challenge

Can you find the best bridge-building shapes?

Procedure

❶ Using paper fasteners or plastic ties to connect the tongue depressors or craft sticks, build the shapes shown in the table on the next page.

❷ Examine each of the wooden shapes. Do not take the shapes apart, and be careful not to break them.

❸ Try to change the original shapes by pushing or pulling gently.

? *Draw the new shapes you create in the table on the next page.*

? *Which shapes changed least? Which shapes would you use as part of a bridge? Would you stand under a bridge made from those shapes?*

_____

_____

_____

_____

_____

_____

New Wooden Shapes	
Original Shape	Draw the new shapes you create.

Teacher Notes for the Science Activity

Materials

Per class
- drill with a ¼-inch drill bit

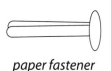

paper fastener

Per group
- 34 tongue depressors or craft sticks
- 31 paper fasteners or plastic ties

Setup

- If you are using tongue depressors, drill a ¼-inch hole in each end. If you are using craft sticks, drill ⅛-inch holes.

Answers and Observations

❸ *Which shapes changed least? Which shapes would you use as part of a bridge? Would you stand under a bridge made from those shapes?*

The triangle and double triangle are the most stable shapes. Triangles are good shapes to use in bridges.

? *Draw the new shapes you create in the attached table.*

See the table on the next page.

Suggestions for Follow-Up

Ask students to look at bridges when they're riding in the car with their parents or on the school bus. Can they see how the designers and builders used geometric shapes in these bridges? Which shapes do they see?

New Wooden Shapes	
Original Shape	Possible Shapes

Assessment

Materials

Per class
- can of soup
- 2 books or blocks of the same size
- masking tape

Per group
- 25, 1-inch potato pieces
- box of round toothpicks
  Have extra toothpicks on hand in case of breakage.

1 inch

Setup

- Cut the potatoes into 1-inch pieces that are approximately cubic. If cubes are not possible, it is acceptable to use the natural shape of a potato. You may want to dip the pieces in vinegar or lemon juice to keep them from turning brown too quickly. However, even brown potato pieces will work as long as they are still firm.

- Set two books or blocks 12 inches apart on a table. Mark the location of the inside edge of each book with masking tape so that the books can be returned to the proper position if they are accidentally moved. Place the soup can nearby. Place a sign at the table that says "Bridge Testing Site."

Challenge

Challenge students to design a bridge made only of toothpicks and potato pieces in which they use as few potato pieces and toothpicks as possible. Explain that the bridge should be able to span two books set 12 inches apart and support a can of soup. Instruct students to sketch plans for their bridges and then build them.

Have groups take turns demonstrating their bridges for the class at the "Bridge Testing Site." Post the plans for the successful bridges and discuss what factors the successful designs have in common. Record the number of toothpicks and potatoes used by each group. Do more toothpicks and potatoes necessarily mean the bridge is stronger? *No.* What factors contribute to the strength of the bridge? *Design, shape, and structure.*

Have students try to apply variations of the successful designs to create bridges that span 15 inches and support a can of soup. After testing the new bridges, have students write one important fact or idea they learned in this lesson in their science journals.

Science Explanation

This section explains the science concepts in this lesson as well as in the "Under Construction" Family Science Challenge in Science Night Family Fun from A to Z. *It is intended for the teacher's information and may be modified as necessary for discussion with students.*

During the Family Science Challenge, family teams will probably discover that folding the paper bridge can dramatically affect the number of pennies it can support. The original paper bridge will not hold much weight because it is very flexible. All the downward force due to gravity is centered directly under the pennies. Folding the paper in half makes it more rigid and distributes the downward force along its length, thus increasing the strength, but not by much. Folding the sides of the paper up (see Figure 1) to make a bridge with sides increases the strength further. The amount of the increase depends upon the relative size of the sides. Making multiple folds to pleat the bridge further increases its strength. The number and spacing of folds usually determines the strength. This multiple-fold shape is similar to what is observed within the corrugated cardboard. The triangles formed in each case are very strong, and a great deal of weight is needed to deform them and collapse the bridge.

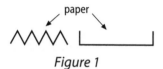

Figure 1

Of the geometric shapes tested in the classroom Science Activity, the triangle and double triangles are the most resistant to changing shape. This is because deforming a triangle would require stretching (or compressing) it, which is hard to do. So as long as the triangular shape is kept planar, it is very sturdy. This is why the strongest bridges built by the class probably include triangular shapes. An actual bridge uses a truss (a rigid framework consisting of straight pieces of metal or wood) to give strength. Two beams forming a truss are connected by struts, which form a very strong framework when arranged in triangles. Figure 2 shows a variety of bridge trusses.

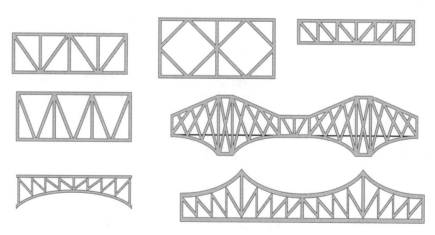

Figure 2: A variety of bridge trusses

Cross-Curricular Integration

Art and Music

- Investigate the history of London Bridge and the song "London Bridge is Falling Down." Sing the song.
- Draw an architectural plan for a bridge.

Language Arts

- Have students write poems in the shape of bridges.
- For older students you might wish to introduce the idea of a key novel, painting, or musical composition that "bridged" eras.
- Read aloud or have students read one or more of the following books:
  - *Bridges Connect,* by Lee Sullivan Hill (Carolrhoda Books, ISBN 1575050218)
    Introduces different kinds of bridges, their materials, construction, and maintenance.
  - *I Know A Bridge,* by Jeff Sheppard (Macmillan, ISBN 0-02-782457-8)
    Soft, lyrical paintings and a quiet, intimate poem celebrate all manner of bridges, from a board thrown across a puddle to a stone crossing just right for two friends to fish from.
  - One or more books in the series by David Macaulay that deals with the construction of historic projects. Titles include *Pyramid City, Underground, Cathedral,* and *Castle.* These books go into great detail about planning, research, and tools, as well as actual construction.

Mathematics

- Discuss the strength of different geometric shapes in architecture. Bring in pictures of buildings, bridges, and towers with a visible support structure and have students identify the geometric shapes.
- Using the book *Bridges Connect,* by Lee Sullivan Hill (Carolrhoda Books, ISBN 1575050218), identify the different geometric shapes that make up a bridge and discuss them.

Social Studies

- Investigate with the transportation department what limits are set in your area for traffic on roads and bridges. How are these laws enforced? Who determines the safety limits?
- Match famous bridges to cities (Golden Gate Bridge, Brooklyn Bridge, etc.) and locate them on a map. Or use the book *Bridges,* by Norman and Madelyn Carlisle (Childrens Press, ISBN 0516016776), and locate the "Unusual Bridges of the World" listed in the book using a globe or world map.
- Research the types of bridges used by different cultures at various times in history. A good source might be *The Story of the Brooklyn Bridge,* by Zachary Kent (Childrens Press, ISBN 0516047396), which compares how bridges were built in the 1880s and how they are built now. Another book you may want to make available to students is *Building the Golden Gate,* by Kathy Pelta (Lerner, ISBN 0822595214). This book describes the planning and construction of the Golden Gate Bridge in San Francisco.

Versatile Inertia

Enrich the **"Vertically Challenged"** *activity in the book* Science Night Family Fun from A to Z *or use as a stand-alone lesson on inertia and Newton's first law.*

Students investigate the role of inertia and friction as they perform amazing feats.

. . . . **Key Science Topics**

- friction
- inertia
- Newton's first law

. . . . **Average Time Required**

Science Activity

Setup	5	minutes
Performance	20	minutes
Cleanup	5	minutes

.... # National Science Education Standards

Science as Inquiry Standards

- Abilities Necessary to Do Scientific Inquiry
  Students conduct simple investigations involving inertia, gravity, and the effect of water on a moving object.

  Students use their observations and results to refine how they perform each task presented and to develop tips for performing tasks successfully.

  Students use their observations to predict what will happen when a new task is performed.

  Students analyze their procedures and tips for each task and those of their classmates.

  Students communicate their observations and tips to their adult partners and to their classmates.

Physical Science

- Properties of Objects and Materials
  Air and water have the property of resistance, which affects how objects, like the pennies in the Family Science Challenge, move through them.

  Objects such as the book, coin, and dowel rod have the property of inertia, which is resistance to attempts to move or change the motion of an object.

- Position and Motion of Objects
  The position and motion of objects such as the coins, fabric, card, pie pan, and toilet-paper tubes can be changed by pushing and pulling.

- Motions and Forces
  Gravity causes the pennies in the Family Science Challenge and the eggs in the Science Activity to fall.

  Inertia keeps the book and the coin in place when the fabric and the card are moved.

- Transfer of Energy
  A portion of the kinetic energy of the pennies in the Family Science Challenge is transferred to the water, which slows down the pennies.

History and Nature of Science

- Science as a Human Endeavor
  Students learn how people have studied and used the principles of gravity and inertia.

- History of Science
  Students investigate the history and development of orbital satellites and vehicles for space travel.

Science Activity

Materials

piece of smooth nylon fabric • thick hard-backed book • trading card or playing card • nickel

Challenge

Can you remove the fabric and card without moving the book and coin sitting on them?

Procedure

Part A

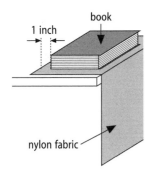

1 inch

book

nylon fabric

Figure 1

❶ Lay the fabric over the edge of a level table and set the textbook on the fabric as shown in Figure 1. Most of the fabric should hang off the table's edge.

❷ With both hands, firmly grasp the fabric hanging from the table's edge. Pull sharply and quickly downward to snatch the fabric from under the book.

❸ Set up the fabric and book again and practice the trick until you can consistently pull the fabric away and leave the book on the table.

Part B

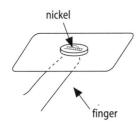

nickel

finger

Figure 2

❶ Have one partner balance a card, such as a trading card or playing card, on his or her fingertip and then place a nickel on it as shown in Figure 2.

❷ Have the other partner attempt to flick away the card so the nickel stays balanced on the first partner's fingertip.

❸ Practice until you are consistently able to knock away the card and leave the nickel on the fingertip.

Teacher Notes for the Science Activity

Materials

For Setup only
• scissors

Per group or per student
• piece of smooth nylon fabric, approximately 1 foot x 2 foot
• thick hard-backed book
• trading card or playing card
• nickel

Suggestion for Follow-Up

Have the class discuss their results and suggest tips for performing these tricks successfully.

Assessment

Materials

Per teacher demonstration
- 2, 400-mL beakers
- water
- large aluminum pie pan
- 2 empty, narrow toilet-paper tubes (Do NOT use the wide tubes from double rolls of toilet paper.)
- 2 raw eggs
- full-sized broom

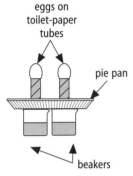

eggs on toilet-paper tubes

pie pan

beakers

Figure 1

Setup

❶ Fill the two beakers halfway with water and set them side-by-side near the edge of a flat, level table.

❷ Balance the pie pan on top of the beakers so that the pie pan extends an inch or so beyond the edge of the table. Move the beakers if necessary.

❸ Set the two toilet-paper tubes upright in the pie pan so that each tube is directly over the center of one of the supporting beakers. (See Figure 1.)

❹ Balance an egg on top of each toilet-paper tube.

❺ Stand the broom upright a few inches from the edge of the table next to the pie pan.

Teacher Demonstration

Push the broom down so that the bristles bend in an "L" facing you, and step on the bent end of the broom. (See Figure 2.) Make sure the broom is aligned with the center of the pie pan without touching it. Pull the handle of the broom firmly back toward you at about a 45-degree angle.

After you give your students the challenge (below), release the handle of the broom so that it strikes the pie pan sharply, sending it moving horizontally. If the handle hits at the right spot with the right speed, it should knock the pie pan and toilet-paper tubes away, and the eggs should fall into the beakers of water.

Figure 2

Challenge

Tell students their challenge is to predict what will happen when you strike the pan with the broom (see the teacher demonstration above) based on the inertia and friction feats performed in the classroom Science Activity. Have students record their predictions in their science journals. After the demonstration is finished, have students explain what happened. Then have students write one important fact or idea they learned during this lesson in their science journals.

Science Explanation

This section explains the science concepts in this lesson as well as in the "Vertically Challenged" Family Science Challenge in Science Night Family Fun from A to Z. *It is intended for the teacher's information and may be modified as necessary for discussion with students.*

The classroom Science Activity and the Assessment dramatically illustrate Newton's first law of motion, which states that unless an object is acted upon by unbalanced forces, it remains either at rest or in motion in a straight line at constant speed. In the Science Activity, the book remains on the table and the nickel remains on the finger if the tricks are performed successfully. According to Newton's first law, the book and nickel remain in their state of rest. In Part A, if the fabric were pulled slowly toward the edge of the table, friction between the book and the fabric would act on the book, causing it to move with the fabric. When the fabric is pulled sharply, the friction force acts on the book for only a brief instant and is not significant enough to move it. Similarly, in Part B, the friction force of the card on the nickel is not significant when the trick is done successfully.

In the Assessment, objects fall straight down when their supports are knocked sideways swiftly enough. In this case, the objects at rest (the eggs) cannot remain suspended in the air when their supports are knocked from under them. Instead, the force of gravity causes the eggs to fall. If the friction force between the eggs and the cardboard tubes is small enough, the force of gravity is the only force acting on the eggs when the supports are knocked away, and the eggs are able to fall straight down instead of being knocked sideways.

Gravity was also an important factor in the Family Science Challenge. It caused the pennies to fall when released. It was probably very easy to drop pennies into the Dry Target but harder to hit the target that was submerged in water, because when the pennies hit the water, they often slowed down and veered in one direction or another. This veering occurred because water resistance is greater than air resistance. When the pennies hit the water, it absorbed some of the kinetic energy the pennies had. The water helped to break the pennies' fall, slow them down, and cause them to veer off a straight path.

Cross-Curricular Integration

Language Arts

- Have students write a book of tricks in which they describe how to do the tricks in this lesson.

Life Science

- Have students research how martial arts experts use quickly applied forces to break boards or bricks.

Home, Safety, and Career

- Have students explain how Newton's first law relates to the importance of wearing a seat belt.

Social Studies

- Have students research Sir Isaac Newton and the time period in which he lived.
- Have students study the history and development of orbital satellites and vehicles for space travel. Have them concentrate on how scientists and engineers used the principles of gravity and inertia to achieve orbit and space flight.

Wacky Treasure

Enrich the **"Wow! Pop This!"** *activity in the book* Science Night Family Fun from A to Z *or use as a stand-alone lesson on acids and bases.*

Students use a chemical reaction to open treasure rocks, and they examine the effect size and shape have on the reaction time.

.... ## Key Science Topics

- carbon dioxide gas
- chemical reactions

.... ## Average Time Required

Setup   20–30 minutes plus three days drying time
Performance 10–15 minutes
Cleanup   5 minutes

 Overview

. . . . **National Science Education Standards**

Science as Inquiry Standards

- Abilities Necessary to Do Scientific Inquiry
Students conduct a simple experiment and use their observations to design an experiment to reveal the treasure in the treasure rock.

  In the Assessment, students plan and conduct an investigation to determine which ingredient in the treasure rocks (flour, baking soda, or water) reacts with vinegar.

  Students discuss their observations and explanations with their adult partners.

  Students discuss what methods they used and why, and they compare their observations and results with the rest of the class.

Physical Science

- Properties of Objects and Materials
The treasure rocks are a mixture of flour, baking soda, and water. The behavior of the rocks in water and in vinegar is the result of the behavior of the components of the mixture.

  Vinegar (an acid) and baking soda (a base) will react to form new substances, including carbon dioxide gas.

250

Science Activity

Materials

2 pebbles • water • vinegar • 2 small plastic cups • treasure rock

Challenge

Can you use chemistry to reveal the hidden treasure in the treasure rocks without breaking them open?

Procedure

❶ Examine a pebble closely without breaking it.

? *Describe what it looks and feels like.*

_____

_____

_____

❷ Pour about ½ inch of water into a small cup. Place the pebble in the water in the cup and observe it after about a minute.

? *Describe what happens.*

_____

_____

_____

❸ Pour about ½ inch of vinegar into a second cup. Place a second pebble in the vinegar in the cup. Observe for about a minute.

? *Describe what happens.*

_____

_____

_____

4 You will now be given a treasure rock made of the same chemicals as the pebble. Your challenge is to find any treasure that may be in the treasure rock without breaking it open. Use your earlier observations to design an experiment to do this.
After 3–5 minutes, you may have to add additional liquid or even replace the liquid you are using with a fresh portion.

? *Record your procedure and the results of your experiment.*

_____

_____

_____

_____

_____

_____

_____

Teacher Notes
for the Science Activity

Materials

For Setup, per group or student
- about 4 tablespoons baking soda
- about 1 tablespoon flour
- water
- spoon
- small plastic cup
- "treasure" such as a small plastic jewel, animal, or other object
- measuring spoons
- dropper
- waxed paper
- (optional) food color

Per class
- waste bucket
- paper towels

Per group or student
- 2 pebbles (See Setup)
- water
- white vinegar
- 2 plastic cups
- treasure rock (See Setup)

Resources

Plastic animals or plastic jewels are available from toy and novelty stores. The Oriental Trading Company (800/228-2269) carries a large assortment of items that would make suitable treasures.

Setup

❶ To make 3–4 treasure rocks, mix 2 tablespoons baking soda with ½ tablespoon flour in a small cup. Add a drop of food color if desired. Add approximately 10 mL water and stir until a thick paste has formed. If the paste is too runny, add a little more flour. If the paste is too dry, add a little more water.

❷ Form the paste into balls and push a treasure into the center of each ball, making sure that the paste covers the treasure completely. Place the paste balls with treasure inside on waxed paper and allow them to dry into rocks. (This takes about three days.)

❸ To make pebbles, use the recipe in step 1 but divide the paste into smaller balls. (The amounts listed in step 1 will make 8–10 pebbles. Each student or group will need two pebbles.) Allow the pebbles to dry as in step 2.

Answers and Observations

❷ *Describe what happens.*

The pebble slowly begins to dissolve.

❸ *Describe what happens.*

Bubbling occurs immediately as the pebble reacts with the vinegar.

❹ *Record your procedure and the results of your experiment.*

Use vinegar to react with the baking soda in the treasure rock.

Suggestions for Follow-Up

Discuss the procedure students used to uncover the hidden treasure, why they selected this procedure, and their observations. Compare results as a class.

Assessment

Materials

Per class
- bucket for waste liquids
- paper towels

Per group or student
- flour
- baking soda
- water
- vinegar
- plastic spoons
- 3 plastic cups

Challenge

Tell students the recipe you used to make the treasure rocks. Challenge students to design a procedure using the ingredients that made up the treasure rocks (flour, baking soda, and water) to find out which of these three ingredients reacts with vinegar to form bubbles. If students are working in groups, instruct them to discuss various ideas before settling on a plan. Have students share their plan with you before they begin testing.

Once testing is complete, let students share their results with the class. Have students write one important fact or idea they learned during this lesson in their science journals.

Science Explanation

This section explains the science concepts in this lesson as well as in the "Wow! Pop This!" Family Science Challenge in Science Night Family Fun from A to Z. *It is intended for the teacher's information and may be modified as necessary for discussion with students.*

The Alka-Seltzer used in the Family Science Challenge is a mixture of several solids, including sodium bicarbonate (baking soda), citric acid, and acetylsalicylic acid (aspirin). When mixed with water, these solids dissolve. In solution, the acids provide a source of hydrogen ion ($H^+(aq)$) and the sodium bicarbonate provides a bicarbonate ion (HCO_3^-). These two species react to produce carbon dioxide gas as shown by the following equation:

$$H^+(aq) \ + \ HCO_3^-(aq) \ \rightleftharpoons \ H_2O(l) \ + \ CO_2(g)$$

hydrogen ion	bicarbonate ion	water	carbon dioxide gas

Even though the solid Alka-Seltzer seems to be disappearing, the matter it is made from is not destroyed but rather converted to other products, including carbon dioxide gas. This is evidenced by the bubbles that are visible as the Alka-Seltzer is dropped into water. These bubbles are full of carbon dioxide gas. When this reaction is carried out in an open container, the gas is released into the air. However, when the reaction is carried out in the closed film canister, the carbon dioxide gas is trapped. As the gas builds up, the gas pressure inside the canister increases until the lid eventually pops off.

In the classroom Science Activity, the baking soda (sodium bicarbonate) in the treasure rocks reacts with the acetic acid in the vinegar. The reaction produced carbon dioxide gas through the same reaction noted above. The flour and water used in making the treasure rocks help to glue the baking soda together and produce a hard, dry "rock" once the water has evaporated. As students determine in the Assessment, neither the flour nor the water is directly involved in the reaction that produces the carbon dioxide gas.

Cross-Curricular Integration

Art and Music

- Like the treasure rocks, Fabergé eggs designed for the Czar of Russia contained a special gift inside. A picture collection and history of Fabergé eggs can be found on the World Wide Web at www.geocities.com/Paris/Rue/4819.
- Scientists were not always able to use photography to capture details of their specimens. Have the class draw the treasures they found inside their rocks. Have them draw the treasures from several different perspectives, including side and top views, and have them label any important aspects.

Earth Science

- Invite a jeweler to speak to the class about how rocks are turned into gemstones. Ask the jeweler to bring in examples of gemstones that are considered birthstones.

Language Arts

- Read aloud or suggest that students read one or more of the following books:
  - *How to Dig a Hole to the Other Side of the World,* by Faith McNulty (Harper & Row, ISBN 0064432181)
    A child takes an imaginary 8,000-mile journey through the Earth and discovers what's inside.
  - *The Magic School Bus Inside the Earth,* by Joanna Cole (Scholastic, ISBN 0590407600)
    On a special field trip in the magic school bus, Ms. Frizzle's class learn firsthand about different kinds of rocks and the formation of the Earth.
  - *Everybody Needs a Rock,* by Byrd Baylor (Aladdin, ISBN 0698710518)
    A poetic look at properties of rocks.
- Have students write instructions telling someone how to reveal the treasure in the treasure rocks. They can give these instructions to a friend or relative along with a treasure rock they make themselves.

Mathematics

- Older students could create treasure rocks in the shape of a cube, sphere, and cylinder that all have the same volume. Have students calculate the surface area of each rock and then drop the rocks in vinegar, timing how long it takes for the rocks to react. Through a discussion, lead students to relate their calculations to the observation that greater surface area equals a faster reaction rate.

Social Studies

- The class can make its own Treasure Rocks to sell as a class project. This activity can be incorporated into an economics unit in which students learn to keep track of their cost, set a selling price to make a profit, and keep books.
- Study how archaeologists remove soil from artifacts.

Just for Fun

- If you have placed plastic jewels inside the treasure rocks, let students make rings out of the jewels they recover as follows: Form a ring by wrapping a twist-tie loosely around your finger and twisting the ends together. Remove the ring, flatten the twisted ends along one side of the ring, and cover the ring with aluminum foil. Use a hot-melt glue gun to glue the plastic jewel to the ring. Allow the glue to dry for a few minutes before giving the rings back to the students.

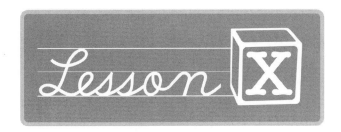

X-pressway Water Racers

Enrich the **"X Marks the Spot"** *activity from the book* Science Night Family Fun from A to Z, *or use as a stand-alone lesson on gravity, cohesion, adhesion, and porosity.*

Students investigate the effect that the slope of a surface has on a water drop's motion and speed.

Key Science Topics

- adhesion
- cohesion
- gravity
- mass
- surface tension

Time Required

Setup   5 minutes
Performance   10–20 minutes
Cleanup   5 minutes

 Overview

. . . . **National Science Education Standards**

Science as Inquiry Standards

- Abilities Necessary to Do Scientific Inquiry
  Students investigate the behavior of a water drop placed on a sheet of paper and on a sheet of acetate.

  Students question why water behaves as it does on the different surfaces.

  Students discuss the behavior of the water drop with their adult partner.

  Students compare the results of their water slide tests and discuss differences and similarities in their designs.

Physical Science

- Properties of Objects and Materials
  Water has many observable properties, including relatively strong cohesive forces and high surface tension.

  The properties of a sheet of acetate are different from the properties of a sheet of paper.

  Students use the properties of water on the sheet of acetate (cohesion, surface tension, lack of absorbency) and the downward force of gravity to move the water drop around the maze.

- Position and Motion of Objects
  The position of the water drop can be changed by pushing or pulling. In this activity, gravity pulls on the water drop when the maze is tilted.

  Students investigate the effect that the slope of the water slide has on the water drop's motion and speed.

Science and Technology

- Abilities of Technological Design
  Students design and test a water slide and make changes to improve their design.

  Students work together to make several water slides and evaluate which slide is fastest.

Classroom Science from Ⓐ to Ⓩ

Science Activity

Materials

aluminum foil • scissors • books of different heights and widths
• plastic plate • dropper • tape or paper clips • cup of colored
water • stopwatch or other timer with a second hand • pencil
• ¼-teaspoon measure

Challenge

As a team, design a water slide.

Procedure

❶ Cut a 1½-foot piece of aluminum foil for a "path." Use with the shiny side up for the activity.

❷ Using the materials listed, design a method of moving a drop of water from the top of the path down to a plastic plate. (Keep the path length at 1½ feet.) Try some of your ideas to see if they work. (The drop may need a slight nudge with the tip of the dropper to start it rolling, but don't touch it again once it starts.)

? *Draw the setup that gave the best results on the back of this handout.*

❸ Now try the challenge using ¼ teaspoon water instead of a drop. Time this trial and record your result in the table at left. Repeat three times, recording the result of each trial.

? *Why did using different amounts of water give different results?*

_____

_____

_____

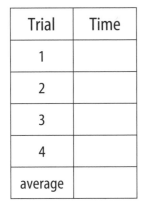

Trial	Time
1	
2	
3	
4	
average	

Teacher Notes for the Science Activity

Materials

Per pair or small group
- aluminum foil
- scissors
- books of different heights and widths
- plastic plate
- dropper
- tape or paper clips
- cup of colored water
- stopwatch or other timer with a second hand
- pencil
- ¼-teaspoon measure

Tips

- The standard width of aluminum foil is 12 inches. The activity works just as well using a narrower piece of foil for a path. If you wish to conserve materials, cut the 1½-foot long pieces of aluminum foil in half lengthwise to make two 6-inch-wide pieces.

Answers and Observations

❷ *Draw your setup in the space to the left.*

The students' setups will probably look similar to the one shown below.

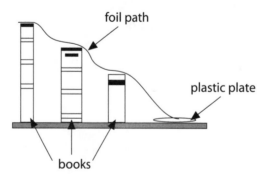

❸ *Why did using different amounts of water give different results?*

Increasing the amount of water to ¼ teaspoon increases the rate of flow down the path.

Suggestions for Follow-Up

As a class, compare results for each step of the activity. Discuss the similarities and differences in the designs that produced the fastest results.

Assessment

Materials

Per student or group
- books of different heights and widths
- waxed paper
- plastic wrap
- aluminum foil
- ¼-teaspoon measure
- tape or paper clips
- cup of colored water
- stopwatch or other timer with a second hand

Challenge

Challenge students to design an experiment to determine whether waxed paper, plastic wrap, or aluminum foil makes the best slide track. The best slide track will be the one on which ¼ teaspoon water travels fastest down the track. Students may work individually or in groups.

Discuss the importance of controlling variables. What variables will students need to control? *Track shape, track slope, and drop size.* How will students keep the track shape consistent with these three very different materials?

Have students record in their science journals the procedures they used and the results they found. Discuss the experiments and results as a class. Have students write one important fact or idea they learned during this lesson in their science journals.

Science Explanation

This section explains the science concepts in this lesson as well as in the "X Marks the Spot" Family Science Challenge in Science Night Family Fun from A to Z. *It is intended for the teacher's information and may be modified as necessary for discussion with students.*

Both the Family Science Challenge and the classroom Science Activity deal with the tendency of water to form dome-shaped drops and for these drops to stay together even when they are sliding or rolling around on a non-absorbent surface. Cohesion is the force that holds a material together. Water has a very high cohesive force, which means there is a very strong attraction between water molecules. This strong cohesive force helps to hold the water drop together as it slides around the waxed paper and acetate sheet in the Family Science Challenge and down the ramps in the classroom Science Activity and Assessment. This cohesive force also causes a water drop to have the characteristic dome shape. The water molecules on the surface of the water drop are strongly attracted to the other water molecules that are next to them. The downward and sideways attraction of the molecules creates a constant pull on the surface molecules, causing surface tension. (See figure.)

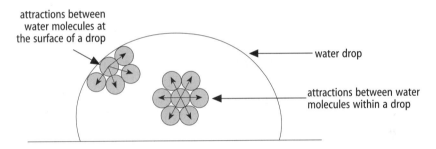

These activities also illustrated another interesting property of water—it is absorbed by paper but not by the acetate sheet, aluminum foil, waxed paper, or plastic wrap. This difference results from the fact that paper is porous and the other materials are not. The porous nature of paper allows the water to be absorbed into it. Also, the water is attracted to the paper by a force called adhesion. The adhesive force between water and the other materials is weak.

While porosity and cohesive and adhesive forces determine whether or not the water is absorbed, it is the force of gravity that causes the water drop to move down tilted or sloped surfaces. Gravitational force is always directed downward. On a sloped, waterproof surface, increasing the volume of water from one drop to ¼ teaspoon increases the rate of flow down the path. This is because the gravitational force acting on the larger amount of water increases in direct proportion to the increase in mass, while the frictional force (between the water and the surface) does not increase as much.

Cross-Curricular Integration

Art and Music

- Create a design using food color. Use a dropper to place drops of the food color on waxed paper and a toothpick to arrange them into a design. Transfer the design to porous paper by dropping white construction paper directly over the design. Leave the papers together until all the color has been absorbed by the porous paper and then separate.
- Play Handel's "Water Music" and have students paint with watercolors on plastic and then transfer the design by blotting with paper.

Language Arts

- Write your own myth or short story about a maze or someone trapped in a maze.
- Read aloud or have students read one or more of the following books:
  - *Mythology,* by Edith Hamilton (New American Library, ISBN 0451628039)
    This book includes the Greek myth of the Minotaur and the labyrinth.
  - *A Drop of Water,* by Walter Wick (Scholastic, ISBN 0590221973)
    This book explains the properties of water, including surface tension.
  - *A Drop of Water and a Million More,* by Pauline Cartwright (Wright, ISBN 0780206436)
    This book tells the story of the water cycle from the point of view of a drop of water.

Mathematics

- Measure the distance a drop travels on the race course. For more advanced students, divide the distance by the average time of travel to get the average speed.

Social Studies

- Research the use of mazes or labyrinths in various civilizations and contexts. For example, many gardens have bushes or shrubbery arranged in maze-like patterns, a tradition that began in Europe during the Baroque period (17th century). A good example of these gardens is at Hampton Court Palace in London.

Just for Fun

- Build a maze with desks or people. Blindfold a person and direct him or her through the maze with verbal directions.

Yaw'l Come Back

Enrich the "Yellow Submarine" activity in the book Science Night Family Fun from A to Z *or use as a stand-alone lesson on density.*

Students create a diver that twirls as it dives.

. . . . **Key Science Topics**

- gases
- mass
- pressure
- relative density
- volume

. . . . **Average Time Required**

Setup   10 minutes
Performance   20–30 minutes
Cleanup   5 minutes

·············· National Science Education Standards

Science as Inquiry Standards

- Abilities Necessary to Do Scientific Inquiry
Students conduct investigations with Cartesian Divers.

  Students use their observations of the Cartesian Divers to develop an explanation of their behavior.

  Students formulate cause-and-effect relationships about the design of a plastic collar and the twirling ability of the divers as they refine the design of the plastic collars.

  Students share their observations with their adult partners in the Family Science Challenge.

Physical Science

- Properties of Objects and Materials
Observable properties of objects include whether they sink or float in water (relative density).

- Position and Motion of Objects
The position and motion of the Cartesian Divers can be changed by increasing or decreasing the pressure on the system.

- Motions and Forces
As the student-made divers sink, water resistance acts on the plastic collars and the divers twirl.

Science and Technology

- Abilities of Technological Design
Students design plastic collars that make their divers twirl as they dive.

  Students evaluate their designs and make changes to improve the twirling ability of the divers.

  Students share their designs with the class.

History and Nature of Science

- Science as a Human Endeavor
Students learn how scientists and engineers used the principle of density to develop submarines.

Science Activity

Materials

Beral pipet • hex nut • plastic cup • water • 2-L bottle and cap • Circle Template • plastic squares • scissors • hole punch • (optional) small plastic squid

Challenge

Can you make a diver that twirls as it dives?

Procedure

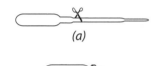

(a)

(b)

Figure 1

❶ Prepare your diver by using the scissors to cut off the stem of the pipet approximately 13 mm (½ inch) below the bulb. (See Figure 1a.) Screw a hex nut onto the pipet stem up to the bulb. (See Figure 1b.)

❷ Fill the cup three-quarters full with water. Fill the 2-L bottle to just below the neck with water. Cap the bottle and set it aside for now.

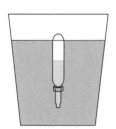

Figure 2

❸ Place the diver in the cup of water. Squeeze the submerged diver to expel some of the air, then relax the squeeze to draw water into the bulb. Release the diver and observe how it floats. Continue adding or subtracting water from the diver until the top of the bulb floats about ½ cm above the surface of the water. (See Figure 2.)

❹ Uncap the bottle. Carefully remove the diver from the cup without losing any of the water inside the diver.

❺ Place the diver, stem down, inside the bottle. It should float near the top. (See Figure 3.) If it doesn't, remove the diver and use the cup to readjust the water level inside the diver until it floats near the top. Put the diver back in the bottle.

❻ Cap the bottle, then squeeze the bottle. Repeat this several times. Pay particular attention to the air that is trapped in the diver.

Figure 3

? *What happens?*

_____

_____

_____

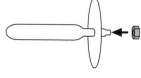

Figure 4

7 Take the diver out of the bottle. Unscrew and remove the hex nut.

8 Use the Circle Template to trace a circle with a diameter of about 2½ inches on one of the plastic squares. Lay the Circle Template right-side-up on the plastic circle and use a hole punch to punch a hole in the middle of the circle. Place the circle of plastic on the stem of the pipet bulb. Screw the hex nut back on the stem. (See Figure 4.)

9 Make propeller-like blades on your circle by cutting six equally spaced notches around the parameter of the circle. Then fold or bend these blades alternately up and down as shown in Figure 5.

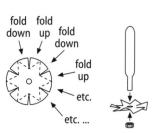

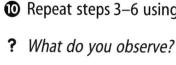

Figure 5

10 Repeat steps 3–6 using the diver with the plastic propeller blades.

? *What do you observe?*

_____

_____

_____

Teacher Notes
for the Science Activity

Materials

Per class
* hole punch

Per student or group
* disposable Beral™ graduated pipet

Beral graduated pipets come in many models and sizes. Model number B78-400 from Micro Mole Scientific, 1312 N. 15th Street, Pasco, WA, 99301, 509/545-4904, is used and illustrated in this lesson.

* brass, stainless steel, or galvanized $^{12}/_{24}$ hex nut

Pipet manufacturers sometimes change the design and specifications of their pipets. You may want to wait to purchase the hex nuts until after the pipets have arrived, then use these pipets to select the hex nuts. The nuts should be just smaller than the pipet stem so that the nut cuts grooves, or threads, into the stem. Hex nuts can be purchased from a hardware store. If you cannot find hex nuts of the right size, you can wrap clear tape around the pipet stem to make it bigger and allow the nuts to fit tightly.

* tall plastic cup
* 2-L plastic soft-drink bottle with cap
* water
* 2, 3-cm squares of colored plastic
* scissors
* (optional) small plastic squid

Small plastic squids, commonly used as fishing lures, may be available at fish bait or hardware stores. Educational Innovations, 151 River Road, Cos Cob, CT 06807, 203/629-6049 (http://www.teachersource.com/), sells a product called Squidy™, which is a Cartesian diver decorated with a plastic squid. Squidys are sold separately or in kits for a class of 30.

Resources

The plastic should cut and bend easily without tearing. One source is acetate sheets for overhead projectors. These come in a variety of colors. Another source is vinyl book report covers such as "Hot Ones" available with school supplies at most pharmacies or discount department stores.

Setup

* Photocopy the Circle Templates sheet (provided) to make a Circle Template for each student or group. Cut out the individual Circle Templates.

Answers and Observations

6 *What happens?*

The diver should sink.

10 *What do you observe?*

The diver should twirl as it sinks.

Suggestions for Follow-Up

Have students share their observations and show the propellers they made. Then let students use a new piece of plastic and design a new propeller that will make the diver turn more times before it reaches the bottom. What shapes seem to cause the most twirling?

(optional) If plastic squids are available, have students remove the diver from the bottle and remove the plastic propeller. Have them slide a plastic squid over the bulb end of the diver, return the hex nut, and repeat steps 3–6. As a class, discuss their observations.

Assessment

Materials

Per class or group
- 4 disposable Beral™ graduated pipets
- scissors
- 3 brass, stainless steel, or galvanized hex nuts
- permanent marker
- plastic cup
- water
- 1- or 2-L plastic soft-drink bottle with cap

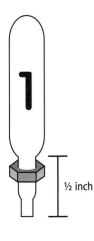

½ inch

Setup

❶ With the scissors, clip off the stem of the pipets approximately ½ inch below the bulb. Screw a hex nut onto the stem of each pipet up to the bulb. Use the permanent marker to number three bulbs 1–3. (See figure at left.)

❷ Fill a plastic cup with water to a depth of about 8 cm (3 inches). Use an uncut pipet to place 45 drops of water in Diver #1.

❸ Test Diver #1's buoyancy in the cup of water. It should just barely float. If it floats too high above the water level, add a few more drops of water and retest. If it sinks, squeeze out all the water and try again, adding only 40 drops. Note the number of drops needed to just float Diver #1.

❹ Having noted how many drops you placed in Diver #1, place five fewer drops into Diver #2 and five fewer than that into Diver #3.

❺ Fill a 1- or 2-L bottle to the neck with water and put the three divers in one at a time. Screw the cap securely on the bottle. Test the divers by squeezing the bottle. Diver #1 should drop first, and the others should drop in order. If they do not, remove the divers and fine-tune by adding or squeezing out a drop or two of water.

Challenge

Demonstrate the divers and challenge the class to figure out how you made them sink in the 1-2-3 order. Have groups of students test their ideas by trying to make their own sets of counting divers. Have students write one important fact or idea they learned during this lesson in their science journals.

Science Explanation

This section explains the science concepts in this lesson as well as in the "Yellow Submarine" Family Science Challenge in Science Night Family Fun from A to Z. *It is intended for the teacher's information and may be modified as necessary for discussion with students.*

Objects either sink or float in water because of their density. Objects more dense than water will sink, but objects less dense than water float. The two divers in this activity are multipart "systems." While some of the individual parts alone are more dense than water and thus would sink in it, when assembled to include air the resulting system is less dense than water and floats.

The divers can move up and down in water depending on the pressure applied to the bottle. When you squeezed the bottle of the Yellow Submarine toy in the Family Science Challenge, the sides of the inner container were pushed in and the air trapped in the diver was compressed. The volume of the diver decreased, but its mass did not change. This caused its density to increase. As a result, the diver sank.

The straw divers in the Family Science Challenge worked a little differently. Squeezing the bottle increases the internal pressure. This causes the gas to contract, allowing more liquid into the straw. The additional amount of water caused the mass to increase, but there was no corresponding change in the volume of the system. The density (which is the mass divided by the volume) also increased and the diver sank in the water. In both cases, when you released the bottle, the air trapped in the diver expanded to its original volume. In the straw diver, this forced out the extra water. This resulted in a decrease in mass of the diver and a decrease in density so that the system was once again less dense than water and floated to the top.

In the classroom Science Activity, the diver system is open and behaves like the straw diver. The collar on the diver is cut into blades that are canted at an angle. When the diver descends through the water, the water molecules hit and bounce off these angled blades. This causes two different things to happen: 1) the diver falls more slowly, and 2) a torque is created that causes the diver to rotate.

The divers in the Assessment seem to "know" the order in which they are supposed to descend. Their progressively decreasing densities determine this order. Diver #1 contains the most water and therefore the smallest air pocket. Thus, it is the most dense and drops first. Diver #3 has the least water and the largest air pocket. It is the least dense and drops last. Diver #2 is in between.

Cross-Curricular Integration

Art and Music

- Listen to "Yellow Submarine," a song about life under water, by The Beatles. Have students draw pictures about what life in a submarine might be like.

Language Arts

- Have students write a story that begins with "If I were in a submarine..." or "If I were a scuba diver." Have them illustrate their stories. You may want them to write and draw on submarine- or scuba-tank-shaped pages.
- Read aloud or have students read one or more of the following books:
  - *The Chick and the Duckling,* by Mirra Ginsburg (Aladdin, ISBN 068971226X).
    Hatched at the same time as the duckling, the chick is successful at imitating the duckling until the latter goes for a swim. When the chick sinks, it's up to the duckling to rescue him.
  - *Who Sank the Boat?,* by Pamela Allen (Paper Star, ISBN 068911373X).
    A cow, a donkey, a sheep, a pig, and a mouse decide to go rowing in a very small boat. As each climbs aboard, disaster grows more imminent until finally the boat sinks.
  - *The Magic School Bus: Ups and Downs, A Book About Floating and Sinking* (Scholastic, ISBN 0-590-92158-4).
    Ms. Frizzle and the class explore floating and sinking.
  - The Wright Group has a series of three books for young children entitled *Is It Floating?, Floating and Sinking,* and *What Will Float?* The text is meant for young readers. Carefully chosen photographs offer good points for inquiry and discussion into the concepts of floating and sinking.

Life Science

- Discuss the pressure in deep water and the effects this can have on living things, such as the pressure in your ears when you dive into a pool. How do animals adapt to this habitat? What happens to them when they change depths?
- Read about how fish and birds move up and down in water.

Social Studies

- Have students research the "bends," which occurs when divers surface too quickly from a deep dive.
- Research the history of submarines and other submersibles and how they work.

Just for Fun

- Invite a scuba instructor to visit the class and discuss scuba diving and how buoyancy compensators and weights are used by scuba divers. Alternatively, view a video about Jacques Cousteau and his work underwater.

Zombie Lights

*Enrich the **"Zap"** activity in the book* Science Night Family Fun from A to Z *or use as a stand-alone lesson on light and phosphorescence.*

Students make their own glow-in-the-dark paint.

. . . .
Key Science Topics

- light
- phosphorescence
- triboluminescence

. . . .
Average Time Required

Setup   15–25 minutes
Performance   15–30 minutes
Cleanup   5   minutes

············ ## National Science Education Standards

Science as Inquiry Standards

- Abilities Necessary to Do Scientific Inquiry
  Students conduct investigations using triboluminescent and phosphorescent materials.

  Students use their observations to develop explanations about the intensity of glow-in-the-dark materials.

  Students use their observations to predict how Gluep with and without activated zinc sulfide will appear in the dark.

  Students develop cause-and-effect relationships about how the time when activated zinc sulfide is added to Gluep affects how the Gluep appears in the dark.

  Students share their observations and explanations with their adult partners and with their classmates.

Physical Science

- Properties of Objects and Materials
  Students observe that some objects have the ability to glow in the dark through or produce light when subjected to a mechanical stress.

- Transfer of Energy and Energy Transformations
  Students observe that light energy can be stored by some chemicals (like activated zinc sulfide) and released over time, and others can convert mechanical energy into light energy.

History and Nature of Science

- Science as a Human Endeavor
  Students learn that people have used triboluminescence and phosphorescence in a variety of ways.

Names _____   _____

_____   _____

Science Activity

Materials

activated zinc sulfide powder • white school glue • small paper plates • measuring spoons • light source • viewing box • cotton-tipped swabs or craft sticks • piece of dark construction paper

Challenge

Determine what ingredients are needed for paint to glow.

Procedure

Avoid ingesting any of the materials used in this activity. Do not use the zinc sulfide "paint" as face or body paint.

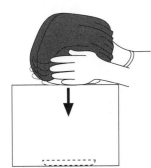

zinc sulfide   glue
powder
Figure 1

❶ Measure ¼ teaspoon activated zinc sulfide powder and pour it in a pile on a paper plate.

❷ Pour 1 teaspoon glue next to the activated zinc sulfide powder on the paper plate. (See Figure 1.) Do not mix them yet.

❸ Set the plate under the light for about 15 seconds, then put the plate in the viewing box, taking care not to spill or mix the materials on the plate. Look into the hole in the top of the viewing box. You may need to put your hands around your face to help block the light from getting into the box. (See Figure 2.)

? *What do you see inside the viewing box?*

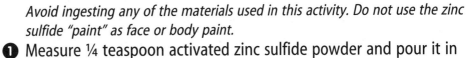

Figure 2

_____

_____

_____

Figure 3

❹ Remove the plate from the viewing box and observe.

❺ Use a cotton-tipped swab or craft stick to thoroughly mix the glue and zinc sulfide. (See Figure 3.) Hold the mixture under the light, then put the plate in the viewing box and observe.

? *What do you observe?*

_____

_____

_____

6 If your glue is not very bright, add just a bit more zinc sulfide, but be cautious not to use too much, as it will cause the glue to clump and crumble.

7 Draw a picture on the dark construction paper with the glue-zinc sulfide mixture and look at it in the viewing box.

Teacher Notes for the Science Activity

Materials

For Setup only
- scissors or utility knife
- masking tape

Per group
- table lamp or fluorescent lamp
- cardboard box
  The box should be large enough for you to put your hands inside and open a bandage wrapper.

- dark cloth
  The dark cloth should be 12–16 inches greater in length and width than the open end of the box.

- measuring spoons

Per student
- ¼ teaspoon activated zinc sulfide powder
- 1 teaspoon white school glue
- small paper plate
- cotton-tipped swab or craft stick
- piece of dark construction paper

Resources

Activated zinc sulfide, listed as "Glow-in-the-Dark Pigment," can be purchased from Educational Innovations, 209/629-6049 (item #GLO-100). Regular white school glue, such as Elmer's® Glue, works well for this activity.

Setup

Students will need a dark place to view the zinc sulfide. Your classroom may offer alternatives such as a dark closet or a table that can be made into a large dark box. You may wish to make a child-sized walk-in "darkroom" from an appliance carton by cutting a doorway and adding a black curtain, as shown to the left. Alternatively, the small viewing box may be made. Use what works best for your students.

- If the small viewing box is to be used, prepare it as follows:
  - Cut the top flaps, if any, off the cardboard box.
  - Lay the box on its side with the open end facing you. This open end becomes the front of the viewing box.
  - In the middle of the top of the viewing box, cut out a rectangle approximately 4 inches long and 1 inch wide. This is the hole students will look through.
  - Carefully tape the dark cloth close to the top edge of the box and halfway down the sides. The cloth should drape over the front of the box. Leave the bottom untaped so students can reach in and out of the box easily.
  - Test the box to make sure it is dark enough to see the emitted light.

- Cut construction paper in half to yield two 8½-inch x 5½-inch pieces.

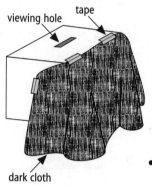

viewing hole   tape

dark cloth

Answers and Observations

❸ *What do you see inside the viewing box?*

The activated zinc sulfide glows, but the glue does not.

❺ *What do you observe?*

The mixture glows.

Suggestions for Follow-Up

As a class, discuss what ingredients were needed to produce the observation. What kinds of products exist that use materials similar to those used in this activity? How is the light emitted by the lights in the room different from the light in this activity? Have students design an experiment to determine how long the glow lasts.

Assessment

Materials

Per student
- 1 tablespoon (15 mL) white school glue
- 1 tablespoon (15 mL) water
- 2 teaspoons (10 mL) borax solution (see Setup)

Per class
- activated zinc sulfide powder
- viewing box used in the Science Activity
- measuring spoons

Setup

Prepare borax solution ahead of time by adding ¼ cup borax to 1 quart water. Stir or shake to dissolve. It is not necessary for all the borax to dissolve. Allow any remaining solid to settle to the bottom, and use only the liquid part for the activity.

Challenge

Challenge students to work cooperatively to compare three different recipes of Gluep by observing them in the viewing box. Divide the class into three groups—A, B, and C—and have students form teams of three with one person from each of the groups.

Have the A students make Gluep by mixing 1 tablespoon white glue, 1 tablespoon water, and 2 teaspoons borax solution.

Have the B students make Gluep the same way as the A students but then stir in ½ teaspoon activated zinc sulfide.

Have the C students stir ½ teaspoon activated zinc sulfide into 1 tablespoon water. Next, have them add 1 tablespoon white glue to this mixture. Finally, have them mix in 2 teaspoons borax solution to make Gluep.
Gluep prepared with method C typically has a more homogeneous glow than that prepared with method B.

Have the groups of three predict how the different types of Gluep will appear when observed in the viewing box. Have them record their predictions and their actual observations in their science journals. Compare results as a class. Have students write one important fact or idea they learned during this lesson in their science journals.

Science Explanation

This section explains the science concepts in this lesson as well as in the "Zap" Family Science Challenge in Science Night Family Fun from A to Z. *It is intended for the teacher's information and may be modified as necessary for discussion with students.*

In the Family Science Challenge, families learned that the light given off by the adhesive bandage wrappers is called triboluminescence. It is a cool light, one emitted without a rise in temperature. It is given off when mechanical energy is applied to certain substances through processes such as breaking, shearing, or crushing. The adhesive on the Curad® bandage wrappers experiences shearing as the two sides move against each other but in opposite directions. Note that other brands of adhesive bandages also have wrappers that give off light, but Curad brand wrappers seem to produce the most light.

In the classroom Science Activity, students discovered that the activated zinc sulfide/glue mixture glows in the dark because activated zinc sulfide is "phosphorescent" (fos-for-ESS-sent). When objects are exposed to light, they absorb some of the light energy. Most objects release this energy immediately, but phosphorescent materials store the energy and release it over a period of time even when the lights are turned off. In the Assessment, the activated zinc sulfide causes the Gluep to glow.

Zinc sulfide does not become phosphorescent until it has been activated. The activated zinc sulfide you used in this activity was most likely activated by heating it to high temperatures (1,000°C or 1,832°F) together with small amounts of copper or other "activators" like silver or gallium. The activators are important for phosphorescent efficiency. Copper-activated zinc sulfide glows for a longer time after exposure to light than zinc sulfide activated by other elements, which makes copper-activated zinc sulfide ideal for use in radar screens and glow-in-the-dark toys and paints.

Reference

Lisensky, G.C.; Patel, M.N.; Reich, M.L. "Experiments with Glow-in-the-Dark Toys: Kinetics of Doped ZnS Phosphorescence," *Journal of Chemical Education.* 1996, *73,* 1048.

Cross-Curricular Integration

Art and Music

- Make designs or pictures that glow in the dark. Phosphorescent media and paints are available at craft stores.

Language Arts

- Have students brainstorm a list of things that glow in the dark and then ask them to pick one of the items and write a paragraph describing the item and what it is used for.

Life Science

- Investigate animals and plants that emit light. A good source of information is the following book:
  - *Creatures That Glow,* by Joann Barkan (Doubleday, ISBN 0385419783)
    This book contains 25 color photos, highlighted with glow-in-the-dark ink, of fireflies, fish and other sea creatures, bacteria, and fungi that glow in the dark.

Mathematics

- Use activated zinc sulfide with glue to make symmetry pictures. Fold a dark piece of construction paper in half, create a glue design on one side, and fold the paper over.

Social Studies

- Discuss how glow-in-the-dark materials are used in our daily lives.
- Research how triboluminescent and phosphorescent materials have been used in different cultures.
- Research the history of television and radar and their use of phosphorescent materials.

Index of Science Topics

Appendix B
National Science Education Standards Matrix

This matrix provides a broad overview of how the lessons in this book and the related activities in *Science Night Family Fun from A to Z* coordinate with the standards in *National Science Education Standards;* National Research Council; National Academy: Washington, D.C., 1996. For more detailed information about how the lessons and activities relate to the standards, see the National Science Education Standards page in each lesson in this book. If you would like to see the complete text of the National Science Education Standards, visit the National Academy Press web site at http://books.nap.edu/ to view a free online version. Since this book and *Science Night Family Fun from A to Z* are designed for all elementary levels, some of the standards statements are taken from the K–4 level and others are from the 5–8 level, as indicated in the matrix. Two statements on one line separated with a slash indicate K–4 and then 5–8 standards that overlap.

K–4	5–8	Lesson	A	B	C	D
		Science as Inquiry Standards				
X	X	Abilities necessary to do scientific inquiry	•	•	•	•
		Physical Science Standards				
X	X	Properties of objects and materials/Properties and changes of properties in matter		•		•
X	X	Position and motion of objects/Motions and forces	•	•	•	•
X		Light, heat, electricity, and magnetism				
	X	Transfer of energy				
		Life Science Standards				
	X	Structure and function in living systems				
		Earth and Space Science Standards				
X		Changes in the earth and sky				
		Science and Technology Standards				
X	X	Abilities of technological design	•	•	•	•
X	X	Understanding about science and technology				
		History and Nature of Science				
X	X	Science as a human endeavor	•	•		•
	X	History of science		•		

E	F	G	H	I	J	K	L	M	N	O	P	Q	R	S	T	U	V	W	X	Y	Z
•	•	•	•	•	•	•	•	•	•	•	•	•	•		•	•	•	•	•	•	•
•	•	•	•	•		•	•		•	•	•	•	•		•	•	•		•	•	•
			•	•	•			•		•			•	•		•			•	•	
	•		•				•			•											
•	•			•			•		•							•					•
									•												
														•							
		•												•			•	•			
			•																		
			•		•		•	•	•				•	•		•	•			•	•
		•		•		•	•	•	•			•				•					

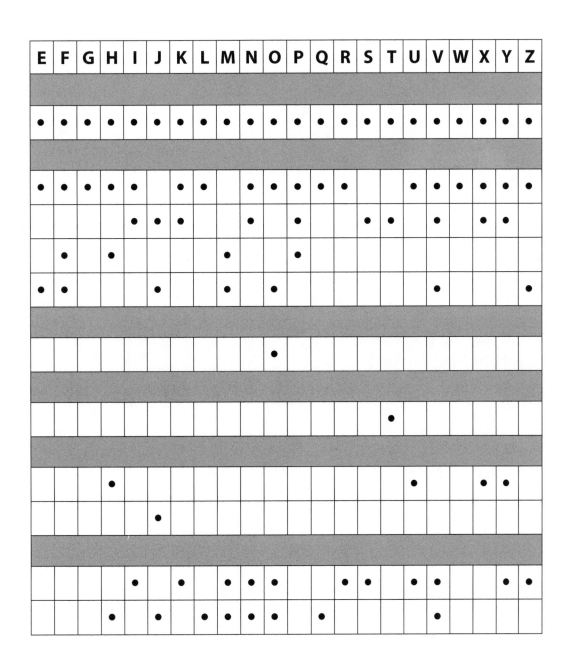